# English Made Easy

By
**Ken Wagner**

with special thanks to
Shasta Union High School District, Redding, California

**EMC Publishing**
**Saint Paul, Minnesota**

Library of Congress Catalog Number:

ISBN 0-8219-0266-0

© 1987 by EMC Corporation
All rights reserved. Published 1987.

Published by EMC Publishing
300 York Avenue
St. Paul, Minnesota 55101


Printed in the United States of America
0  9  8  7  6  5  4  3  2  1

# Table of Contents

# Introduction

Why should anyone have to learn grammar and composition? You may be asking yourself this question. Your English teacher probably will agree with you that the study of English is not the most exciting thing you will ever do in your life. He or she will be the first to admit that not everyone, even the best student, gets turned on by doing exercises with nouns, verbs, or complements. On the other hand, most bright people say the study of English is one of the most important you can undertake.

Probably the biggest reason it's so important is one you may not realize right now. Every time you open your mouth and say something, your listener judges you. Every time you write something, your reader does the same thing. You are judged by how you speak and how you write. When you write a letter of application or speak to a potential employer in a job interview, you'll be judged according to your writing and speaking. If you want to be thought of with some regard, then speak correctly and intelligently. This text-workbook will help you gain the skills you need to do both.

# Parts of Speech

There are eight parts of speech. In this text-workbook, you will learn to recognize seven of the eight: nouns, verbs, pronouns, adjectives, adverbs, conjunctions, and prepositions. It's easy to identify the parts of speech if you remember a few simple rules. Let's look at the parts of speech one at a time.

## Nouns

Directions: A noun is a person, place, thing, or idea. This exercise will refresh your memory about nouns. Look at each word pair and choose the word that is a noun. Write it in the blank. If neither word is a noun, write *none* in the blank.

| | | | |
|---|---|---|---|
| _____ | 1. tree | go |
| _____ | 2. chair | jump |
| _____ | 3. Joseph | was |
| _____ | 4. of | stop |
| _____ | 5. inside | car |
| _____ | 6. you | love |
| _____ | 7. me | lamp |
| _____ | 8. talk | run |
| _____ | 9. give | woman |
| _____ | 10. horse | see |
| _____ | 11. encouragement | believe |
| _____ | 12. disobey | intelligence |
| _____ | 13. rearrange | situation |
| _____ | 14. Elizabeth | passes |

Directions: Can you identify the nouns in these pairs? Remember — if there are no nouns, write *none*.

| | | | |
|---|---|---|---|
| _____ | 15. establishment | clever |
| _____ | 16. war | beautiful |
| _____ | 17. around | Redding |
| _____ | 18. education | terribly |

_____

_____

19. gracefully       democracy

20. horrible       accidentally

# Proper Nouns and Common Nouns

Nouns are divided into two main groups — proper nouns and common nouns. A proper noun names a particular person, place, thing, or idea. It always begins with a capital letter. A common noun is more general. It does not name a specific person, place, thing, or idea. It does not begin with a capital. Look at this list comparing proper and common nouns.

| Proper | Common nouns |
|---|---|
| Los Angeles | city |
| Joe | boy |
| World Trade Center | building |
| Nova High School | school |

Directions: Write all the nouns from the sentences in the blanks to the left. Then use *C* or *P* to show if the noun is common or proper.

Example:    <u>Mary</u>     <u>proper</u>     1. Mary told her sister to leave the dog alone.

            <u>sister</u>     <u>common</u>

            <u>dog</u>     <u>common</u>

**Noun**               **C-P**

_____  _____    1. That town is Sacramento.

_____  _____

_____  _____    2. Dana should have stopped at the big grocery store.

_____  _____

_____  _____    3. Abraham Lincoln awarded the medal.

_____  _____

_____  _____    4. Sarah gave the boy a dollar.

_____  _____

_____  _____    5. John sat in the wrong section of the bleachers at the game.

_____  _____

_____  _____

_____  _____    6. Debbie saw her teacher at the dance.

_____  _____

_____  _____

*English Made Easy*

_____ _____  7. The Redding Art Center is in the middle
                                         of the park.

_____ _____

_____ _____  8. Boston is a big city in Massachusetts.

_____ _____

_____ _____

_____ _____  9. Charles told Fido to stay in one place.

_____ _____

_____ _____

_____ _____  10. Under the oak tree by the river, Dave
                                          ran wildly in circles.

_____ _____

_____ _____

_____ _____

# Pronouns

Pronouns are words that take the place of a noun. Why do we need them? Consider this short paragraph without pronouns.

> Sharon wrote to Sharon's best friend just before the end of the period. The note said that Sharon wanted to meet Sharon's friend after school at Sharon's house. Sharon said that Sharon's mother would be shopping until 4:00 P.M. and that Sharon's best friend could have the stereo on full blast and have the house all to Sharon and Sharon's best friend.

Was the paragraph easy to read? Pronouns, such as "she" or "her," would make it clearer. Look at the first sentence as an example. Wouldn't it sound much better like this: "Sharon wrote a note to _her_ best friend just before the end of the period." How about this situation: You want to say that all the people at the football stadium yelled at once. Using the pronoun "everyone," you can avoid having to name each person. "Everyone at the game yelled."

These words are always pronouns:
I (me, my, myself, mine)        we (us, our, ours, ourselves)
you (your, yours, yourself)
he (him, his, himself)          she (her, hers, herself)
it (its, itself)                they (them, their, theirs, themselves)
who, whom, whose, anybody, everybody, everyone, anything, everything,
nothing, nobody, none, no one, somebody, someone

These words are often pronouns:
which, that, this, these, those, all, each, either, many, few, most, neither, several,
some, one, both

Directions: Complete the exercise below by filling in the blanks. This exercise is based on the information about pronouns.

1. Pronouns are words that take the place of a _____ .

2. It would be much clearer in the paragraph about Sharon and the note if the words _____ _____ or _____ were substituted for Sharon in several cases.

3. Rather than naming all the people at a football game, it's easier to say or write: _____ _____ at the game yelled.

4. Words such as *I, you, he, she, it, we,* and *they* are _____ (always, often) pronouns.

5. Words such as *each, either, neither, many,* and *several* are _____ (always, often) pronouns.


Directions: Write the pronouns from the following sentences in the blanks to the left of the sentences.

_____     1. We do not know for certain about UFO's.

_____     2. The man included everyone in his speech.

_____     3. Whom did you wish to interview for the article?

_____     4. Grab a handful of those.

_____     5. LaToya sent her friend a note.

_____     6. Some of the people in the stands screamed as the team scored.

_____     7. Neither of the boys writes well enough to pass the test.

_____     8. I want comic books to read while you are in the dentist's office.

_____     9. I can pull myself up to the top of the bar.

_____    10. Six books were left in her locker.

_____    11. Several of the books were about horses.

_____    12. Hand me the jacket on the chair, please.

_____    13. It fell from the top of the building over there.

_____    14. Has anybody seen my new stereo earphones?

_____    15. Many have climbed to the top of Mt. Lassen.

_____    16. It is not common knowledge.

_____    17. We wrote the whole book.

_____    18. Anything is better than nothing.

4

Directions: There are at least twenty pronouns in the following puzzle. See if you can find them. Read down and across only. Circle the pronouns.

```
R  M  I  N  E  D  S  H  E  D
O  D  F  Y  X  Y  E  T  D  C
P  H  E  Z  W  O  T  H  E  M
E  E  M  Y  O  U  R  E  J  U
N  R  A  B  H  F  B  Y  I  S
Z  A  M  O  V  G  C  S  T  O
O  N  E  Y  K  I  H  I  S  M
I  A  P  O  G  I  H  W  H  E
L  O  M  U  N  T  H  E  I  R
Q  U  S  R  Q  S  R  O  T  L
```

# Verbs

There are two kinds of verbs. The first kind shows action. What does that mean? Very simply, if you can do the action, it's a verb. Ask yourself if a person can walk, run, talk, hit, swim, jump, or see. These words are all verbs because a person can do these actions.

Directions: Find the verbs in the following sentences. Write them in the blanks to the left of the sentences. Remember — if you can do it, it's a verb.

_____ 1. Bob saw funny people.

_____ 2. He walks around.

_____ 3. He seeks out interesting things.

_____ 4. She runs down the path quickly.

_____ 5. He knows a good person.

_____ 6. She tells everyone about the fair.

_____ 7. Joe drives to his job.

_____ 8. He fixes toys.

_____ 9. Molly mends broken dolls.

_____ 10. She rides a bicycle to her job.

_____ 11. He arrived here yesterday.

_____ 12. Uncle Del painted the walls of the house.

_____ 13. The baby sleeps through anything.

_____ 14. She fished in the babbling brook.

_____ 15. I jumped away from the spiders.

_____ 16. We rubbed liniment on the horse.

_____ 17. Stop!

_____ 18. My aunt and uncle live in Victorville.

_____ 19. Nobody shares any materials.

_____ 20. Aunt Dorothy controls the money.

# Linking Verbs

Not all verbs are action verbs. Some words don't show action. You can't do them. These kinds of verbs are called "linking verbs." A linking verb "links" a word toward the end of a sentence with a word at the beginning of that same sentence. A linking verb is often a form of the verb "be."

    Example: 1. That car *is* a Dodge.
               The word "is" links or connects "Dodge" to "car."
          2. The Warriors *were* the champions.
               The word "were" links or connects "champions" to "Warriors."
          3. He *seems* sick today.
               The word "seems" links or connects "sick" to "He."

Here are some common linking verbs:

| | | |
|---|---|---|
| is | may be | must have been |
| am | might be | shall have been |
| are | must be | should have been |
| was | shall be | appear |
| were | should be | become |
| is being | will be | feel |
| am being | would be | taste |
| are being | have been | seem |
| was being | had been | sound |
| were being | could have been | look |
| can be | may have been | smell |
| could be | might have been | |

Directions: In the following sentences the linking verbs are in italic type  Underline the words that are linked.

    Examples: 1. That <u>cheese</u> *smells* <u>rotten</u> .
           2. <u>She</u> *should have been* the <u>senator</u> for her class.
          3. <u>Tom</u> *feels* <u>good</u> about his research paper.
          4. That <u>music</u> *sounds* very <u>modern</u> .
          5. <u>Harry</u> *might have been* a <u>captain</u> by now.

1. Marilyn *can be* a great teacher someday.

2. She *seems* ill today.

3. This spaghetti *tastes* wonderful.

4. Someday, he *might be* the king of Siam.

5. The cheerleaders *have been* quiet during the game.

6. The teacher *is* a carpenter on weekends.

7. This house *must be* a new model.

8. We *shall be* the winners in our division!

9. The universe *will be* our textbook in astronomy.

10. A new medicine *may be* the answer to the common cold.

Sometimes a verb can be an action verb in one sentence and a linking verb in another. You'll have to look carefully at the sentence to see whether or not it links two words or shows action.

Example: 1. Linking: The driver *looked* tired.
Action:  She *looked* closely at her mother.
2. Linking: This milk *tastes* sweet.
Action:  She always *tastes* her own meals first.

Handy Hint: If you can substitute *is, am, are* for the verb, then you probably have a linking verb.

Example: 1. John *seems* happy today.
John *is* happy today.
2. This suit *appears* wrinkled.
This suit *is* wrinkled.
3. These oranges *taste* sour.
These oranges *are* sour.
4. I *look* funny in this outfit.
I *am* funny in this outfit.

Directions: Put an "A" in the blank to the left if the verb is an action verb. Put an "L" in the blank to the left if the verb is a linking verb.

_____   1. George *appears* daily at the club.

_____   2. Her horse *seems* frisky lately.

_____   3. A cold soft drink *tastes* great after practice.

_____   4. The girls' team *looked* sluggish today.

_____   5. The bell *sounds* loud in our room.

_____   6. She always *feels* cloth carefully before buying it.

_____   7. Her father *looked* in the closet for his golf clubs.

_____   8. Let her *taste* this new cereal.

_____   9. Did he *smell* the fragrance of the rose?

_____   10. The odor of the rose *smells* sweet.

# Nouns, Pronouns, and Verbs

Directions: Each word or words in italics in the following sentences is either a noun, a pronoun, or a verb. Identify each. The first few are done for you.

1. Bob and I *were* in the *parade*.

| were – v | parade – n |
|---|---|

2. *Nobody* should be at school on Sunday.

| nobody – pro | Sunday – n |
|---|---|

3. Joe *is* taller than *he*. _____ _____

4. They *wanted* to see the *dam*. _____ _____

5. My *dog* is a rare *one*. _____ _____

6. Delia *wrote me* a letter. _____ _____

7. My wife *planted* a *garden*. _____ _____

8. That *woman* is the *robber*. _____ _____

9. *Somebody was* in the wrong seat. _____ _____

10. I *received your* card. _____ _____

11. *Thank you*. _____ _____

12. *This* was my *locker*. _____ _____

13. *I* kept my lunch in *it*. _____ _____

14. I *like* all my *classes*. _____ _____

15. Minh's *car* is in the *shop*. _____ _____

16. The *game* is Friday *night*. _____ _____

17. We *knew* about *his* trouble. _____ _____

18. The tall trees *stood* above the rugged peak. _____ _____

19. *Central* is a great *school*. _____ _____

20. *I need* a vacation. _____ _____

21. My brother *does* not like to cook on a camp *stove*. _____ _____

22. Jane *traveled* around the world. _____ _____

23. *He shouted* angrily. _____ _____

24. *They left* in a hurry. _____ _____

25. They poured out *their* hearts to *him*. _____ _____

# Subject-Verb

Now you understand three parts of speech: nouns, pronouns, and verbs. Now let's consider a couple of things about sentences. First of all, every sentence, no matter how short or how long, *must* have a subject and a verb. You cannot have a sentence in the English language that does not have *both*.

Next, what is a subject? The subject of a sentence is the person or thing that is doing the action of the verb. All subjects are either nouns or pronouns.

The horse jumped the fence.

Who jumped the fence? The *horse*, of course. So, the *horse* is the subject.

She wrote a note.

Who wrote a note? *She* did. So, *she* is the subject of this sentence.

Now here's something that is extremely important. It is the foundation to all studies of grammar. When determining the subject and verb of *any* sentence:
1. Find the verb by asking yourself "What can I do in this sentence?"
2. Find the subject by asking who or what is doing the action of the verb.

Directions: Complete the exercise below by filling in the blanks. This exercise is based on the explanations above.

1. Every sentence must have a _____ and a _____
   _____ .

2. All subjects are either _____ or _____ .

3. The subject of a sentence is the _____ or thing that is doing the action of
   the _____ .

4. When determining parts of speech in a sentence, the first thing you should find is the _____
   _____ by asking yourself what you can do in the sentence.

5. The second thing you find in a sentence is the _____ by asking who or
   what is doing the action of the verb.

# Subjects and Verbs

Directions: In the following sentences, identify the subject and the very by writing each in the blanks to the left. In the third blank, tell whether the subject is a noun or a pronoun.

_____ (verb)          1. My mother made a quilt for the fair.

_____ (subject)

_____ (noun or pronoun)

_____ (verb)          2. She used old pieces of cloth.

_____ (subject)

_____ (noun or pronoun)

_____ (verb)          3. My grandmother thinks it's a really
                                    beautiful work of art.
_____ (subject)

_____ (noun or pronoun)

_____ (verb)          4. We all like the quilt very much.

_____ (subject)

_____ (noun or pronoun)

_____ (verb)          5. My mother is very talented.

_____ (subject)

_____ (noun or pronoun)

_____   (verb)                    6. No one around our house is that
_____   (subject)                    talented.
_____   (noun or pronoun)

_____   (verb)                    7. You should see all mother's works
_____   (subject)                    of art.
_____   (noun or pronoun)

_____   (verb)                    8. I am proud to have such a mother.
_____   (subject)
_____   (noun or pronoun)

Directions: In the following sentences, underline the verb twice and the subject once.

Example: <u>Anna</u> <u>likes</u> the warm weather in California.

1. The setting sun made a beautiful picture.
2. A trip through the woods is always fun.
3. The little boy looked at the puppy hopefully.
4. Last night we made ice cream.
5. My brother polished his new car.
6. Jody wanted a pet of his own.
7. Pets need a lot of food and care.
8. Everyone likes pets.
9. The old dog barked continuously last night at the moon.
10. For several weekends we washed cars to earn money.
11. I cleaned my hands thoroughly in the old basin.
12. She thought of the serene setting back home in Idaho.
13. Palmer High School dances are often very noisy.
14. In high school, students expect consideration as young adults.
15. John did all his work.

# Simple Subject-Simple Predicate

Now that you're able to identify subjects and verbs, let's look at one more concept. The verb(s) in any sentence is generally referred to as the simple predicate.

Example: The kite flew above the houses.

The simple predicate in the example is *flew*. It is the verb in the sentence. The subject is *kite*. It is called the simple subject.

Look at this sentence: A ferocious lion might have scared everyone. The verbs in the sentence are *might have scared*. They make up the simple predicate. The simple subject is *lion*.

Directions: In the following sentences, write the simple predicate in the first blank and the simple subject in the second blank.

Example: A toad hopped onto the lily pad.

    <u> hopped </u> simple predicate

     <u> toad </u>   simple subject

1. Our space program must recover from the tragedy of 1986.

    _____ simple predicate

    _____ simple subject

2. His teacher seems wise in the ways of the world.

    _____ simple predicate

    _____ simple subject

3. Students at our school like the idea of double sessions.

    _____ simple predicate

    _____ simple subject

4. Front row seats are hard to obtain for this concert.

    _____ simple predicate

    _____ simple subject

5. A dark cloud hung over the mountains all day long.

    _____ simple predicate

    _____ simple subject

6. People in the army must walk several miles a day.

    _____ simple predicate

    _____ simple subject

7. Kangaroos carry their young in a pouch on the front of their bodies.

    _____ simple predicate

    _____ simple subject

# Complete Subject — Complete Predicate

A complete subject is a little more involved than the simple subject. The complete subject consists of simple subject plus all the words that go with, or modify, it.

Example: The rainy, windy, stormy night before the stabbing of Julius Caesar was a warning of the events to come.

The simple subject is *night*. Now try to figure out which words in the sentence seem to go with *night*. What kind of night was it? Rainy, windy, and stormy. These words certainly go with night. Which night? The night before the stabbing of Julius Caesar. These words also go with night. So, all the words attached to night (including "the") make up what is known as the complete subject.

Look at the verb or simple predicate in that same sentence. It is *was*. The complete predicate, then, consists of all the words that seem to go with or modify *was*. Was what? A warning of the events to come. These words, including *was*, make up the complete predicate.

Directions: In the following exercise, draw one line under the complete subject and two lines under the complete verb. Then put a check (✓) over the simple subject and simple predicate.

Example: A deafening noise from the back of the room could be heard echoing off the walls of the metal building .

1. Shades of the morning sun could be seen above the eastern horizon.

2. The galloping, prancing, snorting stallion raced across the green pasture and into the big, red barn.

3. Clusters of stars in the heavens above filled the eyes of the excited youngsters at the planetarium.

4. Thundering herds of elephants frightened the natives in the village.

5. Taller than the rest of the boys, Herb stood out plainly in his third grade picture.

6. Long, slender fingers raced rapidly across the ivory keyboard.

7. Green, foamy waves laden with seaweed crashed heavily onto the sturdy, compact mass of sand on the beach.

8. A load almost too heavy to bear was strapped to the young climbers backs with sturdy, but thin, ropes.

9. He stepped backward into the unlighted hallway.

10. Stick figures of hard, red clay stood vigil over the young child's toys on the floor below.

# Adjectives

Nouns, pronouns, and verbs — they are the heart of a sentence. Adjectives, adverbs, and prepositions add extra meaning to a sentence. Adjectives describe nouns and pronouns.

Example: dog    This word is a noun. It's a thing. But, let's say more about the dog. We don't really know anything about it. Let's add more meaning with adjectives.

Directions: Fill in the blanks in front of the word *dog* with adjectives.

_____

_____

_____          dog

_____

_____

Directions: Now do the same thing with a pronoun. Describe it. Fill in the blanks with words that will describe the pronoun "he."

He is    _____

           _____

           _____

           _____

           _____

Adjectives answer three questions about nouns and pronouns: *which one?*, *what kind?*, or *how many?*

    Examples: The girls went home early. (Which girls?) The *tall* girls went home early.
                   He sold a house last week. (What kind of house?) He sold a *doll* house last week.
                   There were boys on the team. (How many boys?) There were *nine* boys on the team.

    Handy Hint: If you can put *very* in front of a word, that word is probably an adjective.

Directions: Fill in the blanks below. This exercise is based on the explanation of adjectives that you have just covered. Look back at that explanation if necessary.

1. Adjectives described _____ and _____ .

2. Adjectives answer _____ questions.

3. One of those questions is "_____ one?"

4. Another question is "how _____ ?"

5. And still another of the questions that adjectives answer is "_____ kind?"

6. If you can put "_____" in front of a word, then that word is probably an adjective.

Directions: In the following exercise, identify the adjectives in each sentence and write them in the blanks to the left.

_____     1. My father rebuilds old cars.

_____     2. My little puppy barks at the passing cars.

_____     3. Football is Joe's main interest.

_____     4. I use a big net when I catch huge fish.

_____     5. Big trucks make loud noises.

_____     6. Trout can be found in swift, clear, running water.

_____     7. I use funny, feathered hooks to catch trout.

_____     8. Lisa likes old music.

_____     9. She listens to the music on her new stereo.

_____     10. Rafael likes rare, foreign coins.

Bonus Exercise:    _____     1. The man is old.

                        _____     2. She is pretty.

Directions: In the following exercise, all the adjectives are in italics. Draw an arrow from each adjective to the noun it describes.

Example: *Three excited* girls jumped eagerly.

The boy is *strong*.

1. *Noisy* crowds gathered at the gate.

2. The *beautiful* butterfly made the *whole* forest seem alive.

3. Kate found a *diamond* ring under a *park* bench.

4. The receptionist at the *main* entrance answered the phone.

5. *Last* winter, I made friends with a *ski* instructor.

6. A *large* snake curled around the *warm* post.

7. A lightning storm raged over the *arid* desert.

8. The *cold, foggy* night was *damp*.

9. *Twelve angry* fans shouted at the *unperturbed* official.

10. *That* building is *huge*.

# One Final Note

The words *a*, *an*, and *the* are always adjectives. They may be called "determiners" or "articles." They are, in fact, both of these. They are adjectives when labeling them as a part of speech.

Directions: Write two nouns that you could describe correctly with each of the following adjectives:

1. smart       smart student       smart dog

2. grave       _____       _____

3. beautiful       _____       _____

4. bright       _____       _____

5. clever       _____       _____

6. quiet       _____       _____

7. lovely       _____       _____

8. rough       _____       _____

9. large       _____       _____

10. brave       _____       _____

11. handsome       _____       _____

Directions: Write two adjectives that might describe each of the following words: (Use each of the adjectives only once. Don't use words that are too simple — big or little, for example. Be clever.)

1. book       good book       old book

2. city       _____       _____

3. road _____ _____

4. sky _____ _____

5. wind _____ _____

6. mountain _____ _____

7. house _____ _____

8. day _____ _____

9. lesson _____ _____

10. sea _____ _____

11. cloud _____ _____

12. apple _____ _____

13. poem _____ _____

14. trip _____ _____

15. lawn _____ _____

16. night _____ _____

17. chair _____ _____

# Adverbs

By definition, an adverb describes verbs, adjectives, and other adverbs. It answers five questions: *when, where, how, why,* and *to what extent.*

There are some rules that help make identifying adverbs easier. First of all, here are some words that are *always* adverbs: *very, somewhat, quite, rather, too, soon, really, always, never, sometimes, not.* Next, remember that adverbs generally end in "ly." Not all words that end in "ly" will be adverbs, but this rule works most of the time.

Directions: In the exercise below, supply an adverb to describe each of the verbs. Do not use the same adverb twice. Do *not* use *slowly.*

swim _____

jump _____

speak _____

dream _____

work _____

scream _____

step _____

mix _____

Directions: The exercise below is based on what you just learned about adverbs. Fill in the blanks with the correct answers. You can look back if you need to.

1. Words such as *not, very, somewhat, rather, too, soon, really, always, never,* and *sometimes* are always

   _____ .

2. Adverbs generally end in _____ .

3. Not all words that end in "ly" are _____ , but you'll be right most of the time.

4. By definition, an adverb describes _____ , _____

   _____ , and other _____ .

5. They answer _____ _____: _____

   _____ _____ , _____

   and _____ .

6. *Run slowly.* Which question is answered about *run* with the adverb *slowly?* _____

   _____

Directions: Find the adverbs in the following sentences. Write them in the blanks to the left.

_____     1. The water was too hot.

_____     2. She is very smart.

_____     3. The ride was really fun.

_____     4. We never swim after dark.

_____     5. Sometimes, we like to ride our bikes.

_____     6. Suddenly, she left the room.

_____     7. He walked over the shaky bridge cautiously.

_____     8. The lion roared ferociously.

_____     9. He carefully planned each step of the operation.

_____     10. Dynamically, Wonder Woman lifted the entire building.

Directions: Name the adverbs in the following sentences by writing them in the blanks to the left.

_____     1. I really like to go to college football games.

_____     2. I especially like the large crowds.

_____     3. They can become very noisy.

_____     4. They often have funny cheers that they yell.

_____     5. Some are quite funny.

_____     6. Once, they made a big train sound.

_____     7. I particularly like it when they spell the school name.

_____     8. There is seldom a dull moment at a game.

_____

_____

_____

_____

_____

_____

_____

_____

_____

_____

_____

_____

9. When the team takes the field, the crowd roars wildly.

10. Each play brings fans to their feet instantly.

11. An intercepted pass regularly sends the fans into a frenzy.

12. A long touchdown is extremely exciting.

13. Sometimes, a kickoff can be a reason to yell and scream.

14. Undoubtedly, people come to the game to shout.

15. They can get unreasonably insane.

16. Even the coaches are excitedly nervous.

17. Hot dog vendors occasionally get crazy with the crowd.

18. They, too, yell like maniacs at the players.

19. When the home team scores, the scoreboard lights up dramatically.

20. Finally, the game ends and everyone regains sanity.

Directions: Circle the adverbs in the following sentences. Then draw arrows from them to the words they describe or tell about. You'll find one adverb in each sentence.

Example: You can rarely get tickets for the very best football games.

1. The cheerleaders arrived soon.

2. The crowd followed promptly.

3. Two players quickly took to the field.

4. They hurriedly shook hands.

5. They quickly returned to the sidelines.

6. They awaited the kickoff anxiously.

7. Soon, the ball was in the air.

8. It soared slowly toward the waiting player.

9. He caught it adeptly.

10. Tucking it in carefully, he raced up field.

11. He easily avoided the first two tacklers.

12. The third tackler hit him hard.

13. The ball popped crazily into the air.

14. The crowd stood immediately.

15. They watched the ball impatiently as it spun in the air.

16. Finally, it hit the turf.

17. It bounced uncontrollably on the grass.

18. An opposing player jumped toward it aggressively.

19. He fell on it convincingly.

20. The crowd sat down quite frustrated.

# Conjunctions

A conjunction is a word used to connect other words or groups of words in a sentence. The most common conjunctions are *for, and, nor, but, or, yet,* and *so*. A good way to remember these is by using the acronym (a word made up of the first letters of a group of words) *fanboys*. These basic conjunctions are called coordinating conjunctions. The following are examples of hour each conjunction joins words or groups of words:

1. The boy would not accept the story, *for* he knew the real truth.
2. My mother *and* father work in the same place.
3. I neither smoke *nor* chew.
4. She tensed *but* made the free throw to win the game.
5. I like to ski *or* to fish in my spare time.
6. He dressed moderately *yet* appropriately.
7. She assigned homework on the weekend, *so* the students had to alter their plans.

Correlative conjunctions are the second type of conjunction with which you'll need to become familiar. These are pairs of conjunctions that always go together. Here's a list of correlative conjunctions: *both, and; either, or; neither, nor; whether, or; not only, but also.*

Here's an example of how each pair works:

1. He chose *both* the pie *and* the cake.
2. The cat *either* wants to sleep *or* to play.
3. She was *neither* a coward *nor* a villain in the play.
4. The player caught the pass *not only* with ease *but also* with great finesse.
5. The principal didn't know *whether* Monday *or* Tuesday was better for the assembly.

Finally, subordinating conjunctions are used when you join two complete sentences together, making one dependent on the other. In other words the sentence that follows the subordinating conjunction must be attached to another sentence for support. Look at the sample below.

Example: Although he knew the answer.

This is not a complete sentence. It doesn't even sound like it's complete. It must be attached to another sentence for support. If, however, we dropped *although*, that same sentence would be complete and could stand alone.

Example: He knew the answer.

When we attach *although*, we subordinate (or place below in importance) the sentence, "He knew the answer," and we must attach it to another sentence for it to make sense.

Example: Although he knew the answer, he kept quiet.

So, *although* is called a subordinating conjunction because it makes the sentence that follows it lower in importance than the other sentence.

Here's a list of subordinating conjunctions:

| after | as soon as | since | until |
|---|---|---|---|
| although | because | so that | when |
| as | before | than | whenever |
| as if | even though | though | where |
| as long as | if | till | wherever |
| as though | in order that | unless | while |

Directions: In the following sentences, tell whether the underlined conjunctions are coordinating, correlative, or subordinating. Use these abbreviations *CRD* (coordinating), *COR* (correlative), and *SUB* (subordinating).

Examples:

    CRD      The cows *and* chickens need to be fed.

    COR      She *not only* plays the flute *but also* the piano.

    SUB      I sleep *whenever* I go to the movies.

_____ 1. *Neither* Jim *nor* Jill could enter the race.

_____ 2. She had to choose Samantha *or* Ernestine for her team.

_____ 3. *Before* they could leave the house, they had to clean their rooms.

_____ 4. He had to work Saturday *even though* everyone else was off.

_____ 5. You can't go to the movies *unless* you take your little brother.

_____ 6. *Either* you come home by 11:00 P.M. *or* you'll be on restriction.

_____ 7. *Whenever* he goes skiing, he always takes his wife.

_____ 8. You'll pass this test easily *as long as* you study.

_____ 9. He can't complain *or* blame anybody else for this.

_____ 10. She seemed confused *yet* happy.

_____ 11. Harry is taller *than* Ramon is.

_____ 12. Jennifer watched *as* the plane slowly left the ground.

_____ 13. *As soon as* the train arrives, we'll be on our way to Bend, Oregon.

_____ 14. Wilma doesn't know *whether* to walk *or* to ride the mile into town.

_____ 15. *Both* the girl *and* the boy earned parts in the school play.

# Prepositions

Let's look at the definition of a preposition and how it works. A preposition connects two words in the same sentence by showing the position of one of the words in *relationship* to the other word. Look at the word *preposition.* See the word *position* in it? That's a key word. Look back at the definition of preposition. A preposition is a word that shows *position.* In other words, it shows where something is.

Example: The hat on the table is brown.

Where's the hat in relationship to the table? *On* the table. So, *on* shows the position of the hat in relationship to the table. Here is list of prepositions.

| | | | | | |
|---|---|---|---|---|---|
| aboard | at | but (meaning | in | out | under |
| about | before | except) | inside | over | underneath |
| above | behind | by | into | past | until |
| across | below | concern | like | since | up |
| after | beneath | down | (same as) | through | upon |
| against | beside | during | near | throughout | with |
| along | besides | except | of | till | within |
| among | between | for | off | to | without |
| around | beyond | from | on | toward | |

Here are some hints that will help you with prepositions:

1. If prepositions are tricky for you, first find the parts of speech that you can identify easily. After identifying most words as nouns, verbs, pronouns, adjectives, or adverbs, the unidentified words may be prepositions.
2. Are the words on the list of prepositions? If you're not sure, use the preposition key. Does the word make sense in the blank: _____ the house

    Verbs will fit in the key, but remember the rule for a verb — if it's a verb you can do the action. Prepositions don't fit that rule. Note: Some of the prepositions might sound awkward in the key, but most will work.

Example: *The* the house .............. No
*hat* the house .............. Hardly
*table* the house ............ Not possible
*is* the house ............... Remember "is" is always a verb
*brown* the house ........... Sounds like you're cooking it

Let's review what has been said about prepositions by filling in the blanks below.

1. If prepositions are tricky for you, first find the parts of speech you can identify _____

    _____ .

2. When you're down to just a few words in a sentence that you haven't identified, _____

    _____ that the unidentified word may be a preposition.

3. The preposition key is: _____ .

4. A preposition _____ two words in the same sentence by showing the

    _____ of one of the words in _____ to
    the other word.

5. A key word within the word preposition itself is _____ .

Directions: In the following exercise, write the preposition from each sentence in the blank to the left of the sentence.

Example: _____under_____ The cat is under the car.

| | |
|---|---|
| _____ | 1. The dog is under the house. |
| _____ | 2. The plane is over the house. |
| _____ | 3. The mouse is in the house. |
| _____ | 4. The mouse is in the attic. |
| _____ | 5. The mouse is below the roof. |
| _____ | 6. The roof is above the house. |
| _____ | 7. The roof is beneath the sky. |
| _____ | 8. Limitless space is beyond the sky. |
| _____ | 9. Humans have traveled into limitless space. |
| _____ | 10. Much has been written about humans. |
| _____ | 11. We learn much by our writings. |
| _____ | 12. Our language is among our great gifts. |
| _____ | 13. We cannot function without language. |
| _____ | 14. The study of English concerns language. |

Sometimes a sentence starts with a preposition:

Examples: *Under* the house, the dog barked loudly.
*Over* the house, the plane flew.
*Among* our great gifts, language rates first.

Some sentences or words require certain prepositions.

Examples: Someone arrives *in* a large city and *at* a small place.
Someone agrees *to* a thing and *with* a person.
Someone may be angry *at* a thing and *with* a person.
*Between* refers to two; *among* refers to three or more.
*Into* means entrance; *in* means inside of.
*Besides* means in addition to; *beside* means at (by) the side of, next to.
Someone parts *from* a person and *with* a thing.

Directions: Circle the correct word.

1. An argument began (between, among) the three girls.

2. The soldiers went (in, into) the forested zone.

3. The path goes (beside, besides) the lake for quite a distance.

4. There should be no differences (between, among) two brothers.

5. Did he sit (beside, besides) the girl?

6. The deer ran (in, into) the forest with its mate.

7. (Beside, Besides) the coach, there were thirty players in the room.

8. Mr. Jones has arrived (in, at) Denver.

9. The dog crawled (in, into) its house.

10. Mrs. Jones arrived (in, at) the park at 8:00 P.M.

11. Each of us agreed (to, with) selling snow cones at the game.

12. Cheryl ran (beside, besides) Kiki in the race.

13. Ted has been (at, to) the store for a long time.

14. She knew him as soon as he came (in, into) the light through the trees.

15. The girls ran (in, into) the dugout after the game.

16. The men jumped (in, into) the foxhole.

17. He opened the door and leaped (in, into) the crowded gym.

18. None of us was happy (at, with) the decision about our trip.

19. They slept here (beside, besides) the fire.

20. The pie was divided (between, among) the two hungry men.

21. She is disgruntled (at, with) her choice.

22. The money was divided (between, among) the six survivors.

23. We shared the drink (between, among) the five children.

24. Jane split the donation (between, among) the two clubs.

25. Lucky Luke did not wish to part (from, with) his fortune.

26. Caleb consented (to, with) the choice of the committee.

Directions: Write five original sentences according to the instructions below.

1. Write a sentence that begins with a preposition.

_____

_____

2. Write a sentence using two prepositions.

_____

_____

3. Write a sentence using "but" as a preposition.

_____

_____

4. Write a sentence using "like" as a preposition.

_____

_____

5. Write a sentence using either "among" or "between" correctly.

_____

_____

# Prepositional Phrases

A prepositional phrase is a group of words that begins with a preposition and ends with the first noun or pronoun that follows that preposition. The noun or pronoun that follows the preposition is called the *object* of the preposition.

Example: The cow jumped over the moon.
preposition — *over*
the first noun or pronoun after that preposition — *moon*
prepositional phrase — *over the moon.*
object of the preposition — *moon*

A prepositional phrase can act as an adjective or an adverb in a sentence.

Directions: Fill in the blanks below. Look back at the explanation of prepositional phrases if you're stumped.

1. A prepositional phrase is a group of _____ that begins with a _____
   _____ and ends with the first _____ or _____
   _____ that follows that preposition.

2. In the sentence, "The cow jumped over the moon," the prepositional phrase is _____
   _____ .

3. A prepositional phrase can be used as two parts of speech in a sentence. Those two parts of speech are
   _____ and _____ .

4. The noun or pronoun that follows the preposition is called the _____ of
   the preposition.

Directions: In the following sentences, identify the prepositional phrases by writing them on the blanks to the left of the sentences. Then circle the object of the preposition.

_____     1. The river ran under the bridge.

_____     2. The train ran on the bridge.

_____     3. Airplanes flew over the bridge.

_____     4. Birds sat upon the bridge.

_____     5. This bridge was popular throughout the country.

_____     6. You could find articles about this famous bridge in many books.

_____     7. This bridge was built before the construction of Shasta Dam.

_____     8. Anyone in Shasta County has some knowledge of this renowned bridge.

_____     9. Its fame had spread across our great state.

_____    10. You don't need a home inside Shasta County for knowledge of the Pit River Bridge.

_____    11. Yes, its fame goes beyond our small county.

_____  12. There were many people behind the idea of such a project.

_____  13. You can tell by the tremendous size of the bridge that, besides the engineers, many construction workers were involved.

_____  14. There may never be another bridge like it.

A prepositional phrase can act either as an adjective or an adverb. If the phrase describes a noun, it's an adjective.

Example: The man with the hat is my uncle.
Prepositional phrase: *with the hat*

Let's take the prepositional phrase out of the sentence. What remains? The man is my uncle. The prepositional phrase tells which man. It answers the question, *which*, about *man*, a noun. Adjectives tell you about nouns and answer *which one, what kind,* and *how many.* So, *with the hat* is a prepositional phrase used as an adjective. Nothing to it, right?

More examples: The lady in the red dress was calling your name.
Prepositional phrase: *in the red dress*

Which lady? The lady in the red dress. Which part of speech is *lady*? That's right, a noun. Which part of speech tells you about nouns? That's right, an adjective. So, *in the red dress* is a prepositional phrase used as an adjective.

Example: He is the man from Snowy River.
Prepositional phrase: *from Snowy River.*

The phrase tells which man. Man is a noun. Adjectives describe nouns. So, *from Snowy River* is a prepositional phrase used as an adjective.

Prepositional phrases can be used as adjectives. You've seen that. Now let's look at them as *adverbs*. Adverbs answer five questions: *where, when, why, how,* and *to what extent*. Adverbs describe verbs, adjectives, and other adverbs.

Example: He set the book on the table.
Prepositional phrase: *on the table*

Which question does *on the table* answer? *Where!* The verb is *set*. Set where? *On the table.* So, *on the table* is a prepositional phrase used as an *adverb*.

Example: The cat crawled under the porch.
Prepositional phrase: *under the porch. Crawled* is a verb.

Crawled where? *Under the porch* is a prepositional phrase used as an *adverb*.

Example: Let's meet at noon.
Prepositional phrase: *at noon.* The phrase answers *when*.

Meet when? *Meet* is a verb. *At noon* is a prepositional phrase used as an adverb.

These are the questions adjectives and adverbs answer.

| Adjectives | Adverbs |
|---|---|
| which ones? | where? |
| what kind? | when? |
| how many? | why? |
| | how? |
| | to what extent? |

Directions: Underline the prepositional phrase and, in the blank, tell whether it's being used as an adjective or an adverb.

1. The bike behind the garage is mine. _____

2. The bank on Pine Street is First Federal Savings and Loan. _____

3. We jogged around the block so we could loosen up. _____

4. At the present time, he doesn't know the answer. _____

5. The conversation about the plans was loud. _____


Directions: Underline the prepositional phrase and in the blank write whether it's an adjective or an adverb.

1. Joe Snodgrass has several tickets for the game. _____

2. The newspaper prints news about the school. _____

3. He jumped into the cold water. _____

4. She bought some food for her cat. _____

5. In the afternoon, we played tennis. _____

6. On Saturday, we are going away. _____

7. The light in the kitchen is burned out. _____

8. She missed the point by a mile. _____

9. He showed us a hole in the fence. _____

10. Through the garden, they strolled hand-in-hand. _____

11. The hail in June destroyed the apricots this season. _____

12. He accepted the trophy with pleasure. _____

13. The key to the house has been misplaced. _____

14. The scoreboard stands near the bleachers. _____

15. The scoreboard near the bleachers is new. _____

16. She carved his initials in the tree. _____

17. The initials in the tree will stay there forever. _____

18. The horse in the meadow is a mare. _____

19. The horse ran in the meadow. _____

20. The clouds beyond the mountains were beautiful. _____

21. He put a note between the boards. _____

22. He moved among the people. _____

23. The boat across the water was a tanker. _____

24. He leaned against the fence. _____

# Putting It Together

Seven parts of speech have been explained simply enough to be easily understood. Now let's put it all together identify parts of speech in a sentence. Take a look at the following sentence: *The snake slowly moved itself under the warm rock yesterday.* Identify every word in the sentence, by naming the part of speech of each. Wait! Don't jump the gun, and don't start out left-to-right by identifying the first word, then the second, and so on. There is a simple procedure to follow. Then, no matter how tough the sentence may appear, you'll be able to do it with out any problems.

Here is a foolproof method to determine parts of speech in a sentence.

1. Ask yourself what you can do in the sentence. That gives you the verb.
2. Next, ask who or what's doing the action of the verb. That gives you the subject. Remember: a subject is *not* a part of speech. Now that you have found the subject, you must decide whether the subject is a noun or pronoun.
3. The next step is to go through the sentence and identify all words that are always a certain part of speech. For example, "the" is always an adjective. There are certain words that are always adverbs, certain ones that are always pronouns, and others that are always prepositions.
4. Now identify all words that are obviously nouns and those that are obviously pronouns.
5. Which words in the sentence describe those nouns and/or pronouns you just identified? Adjectives describe nouns and pronouns, so those words have to be adjectives.
6. Are there words that end in "ly"? Do they answer any of the five adverb questions? If so, they're adverbs.
7. Do any of the remaining words that you haven't named answer any of the adverb questions?
8. Okay, any of the words that you haven't identified by now should be put to the preposition test. Are they on in the list of prepositions? Use the "_____ the house" key. If they fit in this key, they are probably prepositions.

Directions: Name the part of speech of each word listed from the sentence below.

1. He, too, hurriedly divides the numbers in the wrong place sometimes.

**Part of speech**

_____ divides

_____ He

_____ too

_____ the

_____ numbers

_____ place

_____ wrong

_____ hurriedly

_____ sometimes

_____ in

2. Soon she passed quietly around the very last corner.

**Part of speech**

_____ passed

_____ she

| | |
|---|---|
| _____ | the |
| _____ | very |
| _____ | corner |
| _____ | last |
| _____ | quietly |
| _____ | soon |
| _____ | around |

# Putting It Together

The snake slowly moved under the warm rock yesterday. Let's go through each of the foolproof method steps and identify each word,

1. You can "move." So, "moved" is the predicate or verb.
2. The "snake" is moving. So, "snake" is the subject. And, "snake" is a noun.
3. "The" is always an adjective. There are two of them in the sentence. "Itself" is always a pronoun.
4. Besides "snake," the word "rock" is a noun.
5. "Warm" describes "rock," so "warm" is an adjective.
6. "Slowly" ends in "ly" and tells _how_ the snake moved, so "slowly" is an adverb.
7. "Under" is the only word left. It fits in the key: _under_ the house. It relates the snake and the rock by showing the snake's position in relationship to the rock. The snake is _under_ the rock. So, _under_ is, indeed, a preposition.

Directions: Now you try some, using the foolproof method.

Name the part of speech of each word listed from the sentence below.
1. An old cat jumped quickly behind the small bush today.

**Part of speech**

| | |
|---|---|
| _____ | jumped |
| _____ | cat |
| _____ | An, the |
| _____ | bush |
| _____ | old |
| _____ | small |
| _____ | quickly |
| _____ | today |
| _____ | behind |

You may have figured out that the last three sentences were set up for you in order of the foolproof method. In other words, looking for the verb is the first step and the verb was listed first. Looking for the subject is the next step and the subject (noun or pronoun) was listed next. In the next exercise the words you have to identify will be out of order. But, do not get out of order with the foolproof method. It is a common mistake for anyone who has to identify parts of speech in a sentence to start from the first word in the sentence and work to the last word in the sentence.

Directions: Name the part of speech of each word listed from the sentences below.

1. Now the spirited horse prances wildly through the rather narrow gate.

**Part of speech**

| | |
|---|---|
| _____ | Now |
| _____ | the |
| _____ | spirited |
| _____ | horse |
| _____ | prances |
| _____ | wildly |
| _____ | through |
| _____ | rather |
| _____ | narrow |
| _____ | gate |

2. She never bought herself an extremely large notebook.

**Part of speech**

| | |
|---|---|
| _____ | She |
| _____ | never |
| _____ | bought |
| _____ | herself |
| _____ | an |
| _____ | extremely |
| _____ | large |
| _____ | notebook |

**Part of Speech**

Directions: On this piece of paper, supply words for the patterns you see below.

               adjective adjective noun verb adjective adjective noun
Example:    The       big     dog  bit   the      wild   cat.

1. adjective  adjective  noun  verb  adverb  preposition  adjective  adjective  noun.

_____

2. adverb,  pronoun  verb  adjective  adjective  adjective  noun.

_____

3. preposition  adjective  adjective  noun  pronoun  verb  adjective

adjective  adjective  noun.

_____

4. pronoun  verb  adverb  adverb  adjective  adjective  noun  preposition  noun.

_____

5. adjective  adverb  adjective  noun  verb  adverb  adverb

preposition  adjective  adverb  adjective  noun.

_____

6. pronoun  verb  adjective

_____

**\*\*BONUS\*\***

7. pronoun  verb  verb  pronoun  adjective  adjective  noun  preposition

adjective  noun.

_____

# 2 Complements

You learned in the first unit that the heart of the sentence lies in the *verb* and its *subject*.

Examples: Cecilia runs.
Dad works.
The plane is flying.

Take a look at some other sentences. They seem to be missing some information.

Examples: Joan was.    (What was Joan?)
She sold.    (What did she sell?)
Mother built.   (What did mother build?)

The words just listed do not make complete sentences. It is true that there is a verb in each group and each verb has a subject. However, the idea of the sentence is not stated completely. Look at the same sentences with completers (complements).

Examples: Joan was *sick*. (The word *sick* completes the sentence.)
She sold a *car*. (The word *car* completes the sentence.)
Mother built a *snowman*. (The word *snowman* completes the sentence.)

Handy Hint: To find a complement, find the verb and the subject then ask "what?"

## Test Your Skill

Directions: In each sentence there is a word that completes the meaning of the sentence. The subject is underlined once, the verb twice. Find the complement (completer) and write it in the space to the right.

Example: <u>Fred</u> <u><u>threw</u></u> a Frisbee. _____ Frisbee

1. <u>Matt</u> <u><u>took</u></u> his son to the game. _____

2. <u>They</u> <u><u>bought</u></u> tickets yesterday. _____

3. <u>She</u> <u><u>sewed</u></u> the new dress. _____

4. <u>He</u> <u><u>built</u></u> the big house. _____

5. <u>Mr. Muir</u> <u><u>taught</u></u> English at North. _____

6. <u>Leah</u> <u><u>taught</u></u> her husband how to fish. _____

7. <u>Sarah</u> <u><u>read</u></u> the book to the class. _____

8. Next, <u>he</u> <u><u>baked</u></u> a cake. _____

9. <u>Don</u> <u><u>had</u></u> a good idea. _____

10. <u>Mrs. Wentworth</u> <u><u>brought</u></u> a dog to the show. _____

Some sentences need only a subject and a main verb. Others as you just saw, need a complement to make them complete.

Directions: In these sentences the subject is marked with one line and the verb with two. Find the complement and write it in the space to the right.

Example: My grandmother is a great lady            _____ lady _____

1. My dad bought a new car.     _____

2. The car is red.     _____

3. The whole family can drive the vehicle.     _____

4. The car is the talk of the neighborhood.     _____

5. My mother is a new aunt.     _____

6. She also is a grandmother.     _____

7. Aunt Jane has four children.     _____

8. She raises fresh vegetables to feed everyone.     _____

9. My uncle keeps the garden in good shape.     _____

10. His main crop is potatoes.     _____

11. The garden is a great one.     _____

12. The potatoes will be thick this year.     _____

13. My cousin planted a few berry bushes, too.     _____

14. He has picked a basket of berries already.     _____

15. Joe really enjoys a big family     _____

16. He has many adventures.     _____

17. His little sister collects stamps.     _____

18. School life never has a silent minute.     _____

19. He will visit the museum today.     _____

20. The school needs more air conditioning.     _____

To identify complements, find the verb, the subject, and then ask "what?" Whatever answers that question is the complement. There are four kinds of complements: predicate nominatives, predicate adjectives, direct objects, and indirect objects. This may seem frightening, but we'll go over these complements one by one.

First, *all* complements are one of the four kinds mentioned. You'll be learning a foolproof method for determining which of the four any complement is. We'll get to that in a minute. First, remember the order of these words:

subject-verb (predicate)-complement

If you have a complement in a sentence, this is *always* the order in the sentence. You could never have Subject-Complement-Verb, for example, or any other order. It has to be S-V-C.

Here are the definitions of each complement and how each works.

# Predicate Nominative

A predicate nominative is a word that *renames* the subject. It is on the opposite side of the predicate from the subject. That's where the "predicate" enters the picture.

Example: My dad is a plumber.

Verb — is
Subject — dad
Complement — plumber

Dad is what? A plumber. Plumber renames or is another name for dad. What kind of complement? Predicate nominative

Example: Sally is a cheerleader.

Verb — is
Subject — Sally
Complement — cheerleader

Sally is what? A cheerleader. Cheerleader renames Sally. What kind of complement? Predicate nominative

# Predicate Adjective

predicate nominative *renames* a subject.
predicate adjective *describes* a subject.

Example: The house is brown.

Verb — is
Subject — house
Complement — brown

Brown doesn't rename house. It's not another name for house. Rather, it *describes* the house. It is a brown house. Brown is an adjective because it describes house, a noun. It's on the opposite side of the predicate from the word it is describing, so it is called a predicate adjective.

Example: Mike is sick today.

Verb — is
Subject — Mike
Complement — sick

Sick *describes* Mike. It is not another name for Mike. He is a sick Mike. Since sick describes Mike, it is an adjective. Since the verb comes between Mike and sick, sick is called a predicate adjective.

Handy hint: If you have a predicate nominative or predicate adjective, you can often turn the sentence around and it will still make sense.

Example (predicate nominative): My dad is a plumber. A plumber is my dad.

Example (predicate adjective): The old house is brown. The brown house is old. Sometimes predicate adjectives sound funny in front of pronouns that are subjects. In that case, substitute a noun for the pronoun.

Example (predicate adjective): She was sick yesterday. Sick she was ill yesterday.
Sick Mary was ill yeaterday.
I am tall. Tall I am skinny. Tall Joe is skinny.

Directions: Based on the explanations of predicate nominatives and predicate adjectives, answer the following:

1. A predicate nominative _____the subject and is on the side of the predicate from the subject.

2. If you have a complement in a sentence, you must always have this order: Subject-_____

    _____-complement.

3. A predicate adjective _____ the subject and is on the _____

    _____ side of the predicate from the subject.

4. If you have a predicate nominative, you can turn the _____ around and it will still make sense.

5. If you have a predicate adjective, you can move the adjective _____ of the subject and it sounds like it fits.

Directions: Each sentence contains a predicate nominative. Write the predicate nominative on the first line. The write the word it renames on the second line.

| | Predicate Nominative | Word Renamed |
|---|---|---|
| Example: P.S. 38 is great school. | school | P.S. 38 |
| 1. The first class at Lincoln was a success. | | |
| 2. Mr. Asnicar was a very popular teacher. | | |
| 3. The Eagles would have been the winner of game if Moose hadn't fumbled. | | |
| 4. My brother will become a great pianist. | | |
| 5. The spring practice will be a good test. | | |
| 6. Mr. McCasland will be the speaker at the awards dinner. | | |
| 7. Although the youngest on the team, Aletha Jumplinger is the best player. | | |
| 8. Teachers will be the chaperones at the game. | | |
| 9. The game will be the last one this season. | | |
| 10. On the last day of school, Washington students become fine citizens. | | |
| 11. The girl has been a cheerleader for years. | | |
| 12. Tyrone could have been the captain, but he was absent. | | |
| 13. Hill High is a great place to make new friends. | | |
| 14. She was the reason that he stayed. | | |
| 15. Smith High dances are a blast! | | |

16. Mr. Crawford was the coach of the track
    team.                                    _____    _____

Directions: Each of the following sentences contain a predicate adjective. Write the predicate adjective in
the first blank. Write the word it describes in the second blank.

|  | Predicate Adjective | Word Described |
|---|---|---|
| Example: Dad seems angry today. | angry | Dad |
| 1. Computers are not new to the world. | | |
| 2. Chinese people were creative thousands of years ago. | | |
| 3. They were smart enough to invent a mechanical computer. | | |
| 4. In some books, the computers were old in the Chang Dynasty. | | |
| 5. In other tales, the machines were useful in India. | | |
| 6. In still other reports, the computers seemed necessary to that ancient society. | | |
| 7. Most were small. | | |
| 8. Some were huge. | | |
| 9. In China, the people grew concerned about these strange new inventions. | | |
| 10. The emperor was curious. | | |
| 11. This new invention could be dangerous. | | |
| 12. They seemed quite practical, though. | | |
| 13. Remains of the objects seem distorted. | | |
| 14. These old computers are strange. | | |
| 15. Their use seems most odd. | | |
| 16. Not all the stories of computers are weird. | | |
| 17. However, people grow apprehensive at the thought of computers from another era. | | |
| 18. This idea was very helpful. | | |

# Direct and Indirect Objects

An object (direct object and indirect object) is a result of or receiver of another word. It receives or is the
result of the verb. Here are some examples.

Example: John built a boat.
> The object of the building or the result of the building was a boat. The boat is the direct object of John's building effort.

Example: She ate lunch.
> The object of the eating, the receiver of the eating action, was the lunch. The lunch is the direct object of the eating by "she."

Handy hints: 1. A direct object neither renames or describes the subject. That makes it different from a predicate nominative or a predicate adjective.
> 2. Second, direct objects are *always* nouns or pronouns. You'll never get them confused with predicate adjectives for that reason.

# Indirect Objects

First of all, an indirect object must have a direct object. An indirect object is the person or thing to or for which the direct object is intended. Not every sentence with a direct object has an indirect object. To find an indirect object *to whom?* or *for whom?*

Ask yourself two questions:

> Example: She gave him a pencil.
> Verb — gave
> Subject — she
> Complement — pencil

She gave *what?* She gave *pencil*. *Pencil* neither renames or describes the subject, so it is a direct object. Now ask those two questions above and your answer will give you the indirect object.

To whom (or for whom) did she give the pencil? To him so, *him* is the indirect object.

Once you've located a direct object, the indirect object is simple. Just ask those two questions and whatever the answer is will be the indirect object.

Directions: Based on the explanation of direct and indirect objects, fill in the blanks below.

1. An object is the _____ of or the _____ of another word.

2. A direct object neither _____ or _____ the subject, so it is easy to tell from a predicate nominative or a predicate adjective.

3. Direct objects are *always* _____ or _____.

4. You cannot have an _____ object without a direct object.

5. To find an indirect object, all you have to do is ask _____ questions.

6. One of those questions is to _____?

7. The other question is *for* _____?

8. Whatever the answer to those two questions is will be the _____ object.

A foolproof method for deciding the kind of complement in a sentence follows: _____

Do *not* skip any steps in this method.

1. Once you've identified the complement, ask yourself if the complement *renames* the subject. If the answer

is *yes*, then you have a predicate nominative. Go no further. If the answer is *no*, go on to the next step.

2. Does the complement describe the subject? If the answer is *yes*, you have a predicate adjective. Go no further. If the answer is *no*, go on to the next step.

3. If the answer to the two questions above was *no*, then your complement has to be a direct object. Go to step #4.

4. When you've determined that you have a direct object, ask yourself: *To whom* or *for whom* is the direct object intended. Whatever answers that question will be your indirect object. Remember — not all sentences with direct objects have indirect objects.

Directions: Find the direct objects in the following sentences and write them on the lines to the right.

Example: People have discussed the Bermuda Triangle for years. _____the Bermuda Triangle_____

1. Tales of a mysterious triangle in the Atlantic Ocean intrigued people for a long time. _____

2. Some legends say the triangle is a corridor to space. _____

3. Other stories tell tales of a black hole. _____

4. Tales of the triangle reached the whole population during this century. _____

5. These tales described the triangle in great detail. _____

6. This area of the sea has a triangular shape. _____

7. Many ships have reached their final port in the triangle. _____

8. Many have studied the triangle. _____

9. The government of the United States has reached a decision about this area. _____

10. Many people have seen the triangle. _____

11. The triangle sometimes takes many different shapes. _____

12. In 1956, a Navy aircraft carrier made its final voyage. _____

13. It met its destiny in the triangle. _____

14. Many seamen lost their lives. _____

15. Planes have searched the area for remains. _____

16. Searchers have found no clues. _____

17. The triangle keeps its secret locked in the depths of the ocean. _____

Directions: The indirect object of the verb comes before the direct object and tells *to whom* or *for whom* the action of the verb is done. Each of the following sentences contain both a direct object and an indirect object. *Underline* the direct object and *write* the indirect object on the line provided.

Example: Joe gave Sally a ring _____Sally_____

1. Juan sent his dad a letter. _____

2. She threw her cat a dead fish. _____

3. They asked him the question. _____

4. My father served the family dinner. _____

5. The old ones left us great folklore. _____

6. The scout leader gave the boys a badge. _____

7. Jane left him a flower. _____

8. Juliet cooked Romeo some lasagna. _____

9. Mary gave Al a gift for his help. _____

10. Mike sent Chuck a gag present. _____

11. Joyce gave Jim a scolding. _____

12. Mr. Hollahan assigned Debbie the essay. _____

13. The coach awarded the athlete the letter. _____

14. The coal dealer promised the school more coal. _____

15. She told us her secret. _____

16. Miss Duckworth refused him the request. _____

17. The teacher granted us the day to do whatever we wanted. _____

# Putting It Together

Directions: Use the foolproof method to decide what kind of a complement is in each sentence. Write, first of all, the complement in the first blank, then tell whether it is a predicate nominative (PN), predicate adjective (PA), direct object, (DO), or an indirect object (IO).

Example: ___pretty___ ___PA___ My sister is very pretty.

**Complement**      **Kind of Complement**

_____  _____  1. My brother is very handsome.

_____  _____  2. My dad is Big Wally of his Moose club.

_____  _____  3. Susie has been a great leader of our choir.

_____  _____  4. That book is quite popular in our library.

_____  _____  5. We wrote a poem in our English class.

_____  _____  6. A nosebleed gives wrestlers fits during a match.

_____  _____  7. A cabin in the Blue Ridge Mountains makes a great vacation spot.

_____  _____  8. That car of Joe's is rather sad.

_____  _____  9. He is a great performer in the show.

_____  _____

_____  _____

_____  _____

_____  _____

_____  _____

_____  _____

_____  _____

_____  _____

_____  _____

10. Donna gave Mary a note in English class.

11. The IRS gives some citizens a headache.

12. Mr. Sehone was a fine basketball player years ago.

13. Driving fast is dangerous.

14. The batter hit the ball over the fence.

15. That sculpture in the hall was really ugly.

16. That kind of machine is common in California.

17. He bought himself a new match.

18. That motorcycle is a Honda.

# Pronoun Usage

As you learned earlier in the unit on parts of speech a pronoun can be used in place of a noun.

Examples: Fred is walking with Ramona.
*He* is walking with *her*.
The car belongs to Satch and Sue.
*It* belongs to *them*.

Here is a simple list of pronouns:

**Pronouns used as subjects or predicate nominatives**

**Pronouns used as objects (direct and indirect) of verbs and prepositions**

Singular

| | |
|---|---|
| I | me |
| you | you |
| he, she, it | him, her, it |

Plural

| | |
|---|---|
| we | us |
| you | you |
| they | them |
| who | whom |
| whoever | whomever |

You might want to review at this time the sections on simple subjects, predicate nominatives, direct and indirect objects, and objects of prepositions. This review will help you in the selection of the correct pronouns in the exercises that are coming up.

Here are examples of how pronouns are used as subjects and predicate nominatives.

**Subjects**

*I* saw the game last night.
*You* are going to win this time.
*Who* stole my book.

**Predicate nominatives**

It was *she* who phoned yesterday.
The winner of the 200 meter race was *he*.
It is *they* whom you'll have to ask.

Here are examples of how pronouns are used as objects of verbs and prepositions.

**Objects of Verbs**

> Ted handed *me* the book. (indirect object)
> He told *her* a secret. (indirect object)
> The snowball hit *us* on our backs. (direct object)

**Objects of Prepositions**

> The argument is between Jose and *me.*
> In the debate, they were against Anderson High and *us.*
> Sit beside *whomever* you want.

Directions: In the following sentences you have to decide if the pronoun will be used as a *subject* or an *object.* Once you decide that, select a pronoun from the correct column of the list of pronouns. Underline the correct answer and write it to the left of the sentence.

_____ 1. (We, Us) spent hours on the project.

_____ 2. The prize was given to (they, them).

_____ 3. The judge named (she, her).

_____ 4. Some of the people cheered (we, us).

_____ 5. Did you give the tickets to (they, them)?

How do you determine the pronoun in the following?

Example: Arthur and (I, me) found the correct answer.

Easy! Put your finger over *Arthur and.* Now read the sentence: (I, me) found the answer. The correct answer is _____ Try this the same way. (He, Him) and (I, me) have been to the fair. Put your finger over *And (I, me)* and the sentence becomes (He, Him) has been to the fair. The correct pronoun is *He.* Now cover up *(He, Him) and.* The sentence becomes (I, me) have been to the fair. The correct pronoun is *I.* Therefore the sentence should read *He* and *I* have been to the fair.

Directions: Use the simple hint you just learned to choose the correct pronoun in each sentence.

_____ 1. You and (she, her) can't guess the answer.

_____ 2. He told Arthur and (I, me) the story.

_____ 3. Of course James Bond and (she, her) rang Goldfinger's chimes.

_____ 4. This really surprised (he, him) and (I, me).

_____ 5. (She, Her) and (they, them) will write the invitations.

Use the same hint to choose the correct pronoun in this sentence: (We, Us) boys spent hours in the store. What word should you cover? You guessed it! *boys.* The sentence will read (We, Us) spent hours. The correct answer is *We.*

Directions: In the following sentences, choose the correct pronoun and write it on the blank line.

1. Bill and (I, me) went to the spring dance last week.   _____

2. (We, Us) boys like to go to the dances.   _____

3. Why were (she, her) and Joe dancing so closely?   _____

4. (We, Us) music students like to listen to the bands. _____

5. (She, Her) and (I, me) are going to dance together. _____

6. (He, Him) and (we, us) are in the same club. _____

7. (She, Her) and Pedro are going to the game together. _____

8. Barbara and (I, me) are going to see Mammoth Cave. _____

9. Fred and (they, them) are good dancers. _____

10. Sheila and (I, me) will enter the contest. _____

11. Is the present for (we, us) ladies? _____

12. I saw (her, she) and you at the assembly. _____

13. The good looking guy sat next to Sharon and (I, me). _____

14. The argument is between you and (I, me). _____

15. Can you give (her, she) and (I, me) a ticket to the game? _____

16. The message was for (them they) and (we, us). _____

17. That show scared my brother and (he, him). _____

18. Please visit my family and (I, me). _____

19. The secret is just between you and (I, me). _____

20. Bonnie wants to go to the dance with you and (she, her). _____

21. We took (they, them) to the football game. _____

22. Please give Aaron and (I, me) another soft drink. _____

23. Loan (me, I) a pencil, please. _____

24. Everything was exciting to (he, him). _____

25. Between you and (I, me), I don't believe that story. _____

26. Did you bake that cake for (he, him) and his sister? _____

27. After you write it, send it to (me, I). _____

28. He saved some for himself and (us, we). _____

29. Just between you and (I, me), I think she's pretty. _____

30. (They, Them) and (he, him) will play at the school's next dance. _____

Directions: Choose the correct pronoun. Write your answers in the blank spaces to the right.

1. John and (her, she) will speak at the commencement. _____

2. (We, Us) girls like to shop in the cosmetic department. _____

3. You and (them, they) will meet Saturday. _____

4. Martha and (I, me) guessed the answer. _____

5. (We, Us) boys will travel to Burney for the game. _____

6. (She, Her) and Joe took a vacation in Montana last summer. _____

7. (They, Them) are the gifts I want to buy. _____

8. (We, Us) athletes must be in bed by ten o'clock. _____

9. Billy, Bobby, and (I, me) are on the polo team. _____

10. (Her, She) and (him, he) will ready the parts. _____

11. You and (he, him) will be on the same team. _____

12. (She, Her) and Beatrice climbed the mountain. _____

13. Why did you and (them, they) go all the way to Utah to ski? _____

14. (We, Us) girls went to the football game. _____

15. (They, Them) are the ducks who ate all the grain. _____

16. Give this to Joe and (she, her). _____

17. The play was read by (him, he) and (her, she). _____

18. *A*'s were given to Colleen and (him, he). _____

19. Mike likes to flirt with (we, us) girls. _____

20. Her little brother tormented Katie and (me, I) by the hour. _____

21. The bear chased (he, him) and Stephanie at Crater Lake. _____

22. The soprano sang along with you and (they, them)? _____

23. (We, Us) boys always eat lunch in the lunchroom. _____

24. David and (I, me) missed the magazine assembly. _____

25. This disagreement is between you and (I, me) and nobody else. _____

26. We took (they, them) shopping at the Mt. McKinley Mall. _____

27. Are you going to McCloud with (us, we)? _____

28. His *B* in English was a relief to (he, him). _____

29. Between you and (I, me), I think a woman will be our next president. _____

30. Take the message to (he, him) and his father. _____

Directions: Choose the correct pronoun. Write your answers in the blank spaces to the right.

1. She should tell Steve and (he, him) about the trip. _____

2. I can't recall seeing the Smiths or (they, them) here before. _____

3. Jack and (me, I) played golf last week. _____

4. It was (her, she) who called yesterday. _____

5. Ask Dana and (he, him) to go to the party, too. _____

6. It should have been (us, we) in the playoff.  _____

7. (Him, He) and (I, me) are happy about your decision.  _____

8. The program was presented to Stacy and (he, him).  _____

9. You can believe in (we, us) athletes.  _____

10. (She, Her) and (I, me) needed to visit our grandparents.  _____

11. The future president will be (he, him).  _____

12. If (we, us) win the magazine sales, we'll have a dance.  _____

13. You have selected either Sharon or (her, she)?  _____

14. Can you handle both the dog and (she, her) at one time.  _____

15. I'll have to ask my teacher of (her, she).  _____

16. You can't dance without (we, us) girls.  _____

17. Phyllis and (I, me) saw a strange movie last night.  _____

18. It was (he, him) who spoiled your perfect record.  _____

19. I'd like to congratulate your mother and (they, them).  _____

20. Bring Rover and (she, her) with you to the picnic.  _____

21. Neither you nor (I, me) will sing at the wedding.  _____

22. The problem with Roberta and (I, me) is that we are both perfectionists.  _____

23. The Asnicars and (them, they) will be traveling together.  _____

24. I knew it was (they, them) who should have voted.  _____

25. I scolded Bradley and (he, him) for breaking the window.  _____


Directions: Choose the pronoun that correctly completes the sentence. Write it in the blank.

1. You and (he, him) seem to understand very thoroughly.  _____

2. Are you sure it was (they, them)?  _____

3. It was Mona or (she, her) whom I saw sneaking into the gym.  _____

4. No one saw Shane and (I, me) at the game.  _____

5. You should have been watching Sonny and (he, him) instead of Renaldo.  _____

6. He wanted (we, us) boys for ushers.  _____

7. We went to the concert with Candy and (she, her).  _____

8. (He, Him) and (I, me) both went out for guard.  _____

9. When are you sending your brother and (they, them) the gift?  _____

10. Miss Hautala said that (we, us) students were quiet at the assembly. _____

11. Chuck and (I, me) were asked to speak at the coaches' clinic. _____

12. The valedictorian was either Chris or (he, him). _____

13. The package belongs to Hazel or (she, her). _____

14. I like Ron and (he, him) quite a bit. _____

15. You and (she, her) are the finalists in the frisbee competition. _____

16. She had to choose the teacher or (we, us) students for the TV appearance. _____

17. You wanted (he, him) and (I, me) to run for office. _____

18. This decision is between Amy and (I, me). _____

19. (He, Him) and (I, me) knew you would be late. _____

20. Please give (they, them) and (she, her) a letter for us. _____

Directions: Choose the pronoun that correctly completes the sentence.

1. You and (she, her) have been together a long time. _____

2. (He, Him) and (I, me) love cafeteria food. _____

3. (We, Us) boys could spend days listening to music. _____

4. He showed (we, us) boys the tunnels under Nova. _____

5. She noticed Barry and (I, me) in the library. _____

6. You and (she, her) are obviously in love. _____

7. (We, Us) boys would like to do more homework. _____

8. Our teacher excited (he, him) and (I, me) when she said that we could take a test. _____

9. This is (he, him) who will be our next governor. _____

10. (She, Her) and (they, them) are all cheerleaders. _____

11. Lisa and (I, me) are wild about our English class this year. _____

12. She showed Michelle and (I, me) some of her cheerleader routines. _____

13. (She, Her) and her aunt went to Mt. Bachelor to ski. _____

14. Tom watched Scott and (she, her) sing at the graduation. _____

15. They gave (we, us) boys free tickets to the Dr. Doolittle assembly. _____

16. (They, Them) and the rest of the class liked their yearbooks. _____

17. You and (she, her) have seen "The Trees of Mystery." _____

18. (Him, He) and (I, me) were thrilled about reading *Romeo and Juliet*. _____

19. (They, Them) and (we, us) visited the science museum. _____

20. They told you and (she, her) the true story. _____

21. He cited (we, us) boys for speeding on our bikes. _____

22. I made cookies for his brother and (he, him). _____

23. The courage of Kent and (they, them) surprised even their parents. _____

24. Between you and (I, me), I think that hill is too steep for me to ski. _____

25. The principal gave awards to (he, him) and (she, her) at the assembly last week. _____

Directions: Choose the pronoun that correctly completes the sentence. Write it in the blank.

1. Dad said he would take Kevin and (I, me) to the lake Friday. _____

2. (We, Us) fans will be cheering loudly. _____

3. That may have been (he, him) in my homeroom class. _____

4. (He, Him) and (she, her) need to buy a new car. _____

5. I'm acquainted with Ramon and (she, her). _____

6. Neither you nor (I, me) can qualify to get into college prep English. _____

7. Offer Barbara and (he, him) a glass of water. _____

8. Just between you and (I, me), the teachers at Summit are very helpful. _____

9. For (we, us) young athletes, not smoking is a must. _____

10. Either John or Mr. Hollahan will give (we, us) a book called *English Made Easy*. _____

11. Will you help Keith and (she, her) raise a garden this spring? _____

12. (We, Us) girls will give the school cheer. _____

13. (We, Us) teachers get silly after correcting papers for hours. _____

14. Sitting between you and (I, me) at the assembly was Mr. Dangl. _____

15. Mr. Crawford told Sherry and (I, me) to write a letter to Joseph Smith for information about the university. _____

# Antecedents

An antecedent is a word that comes before another word. A pronoun antecedent is a word that comes *before* the pronoun and means the same thing as the pronoun.

Example: The pterodactyl raised her proud head in triumph.
　　　　1. What's the pronoun in the sentence above? Yes, the pronoun is *her*.
　　　　2. What one word comes before *her* and means the same thing as *her*? Yes, the pronoun *her* refers back to *pterodactyl*.
　　　　That means *pterodactyl* is the antecedent of the pronoun *her*.

Example: The students rioted, and the police arrested them. Two questions:
　　　　1. Which word is a pronoun? *them*
　　　　2. Who does *them* refer back to? *students*

Thus, *students* is the *antecedent* of the pronoun *them*. *Ante* means "before." *Ced* means "moves" or "comes." *Ent* means "one that."
Antecedent means *one that comes before*. An antecedent always comes before the pronoun the means the same.

Example: The flower lost its petals.
　　　　1. Which word is a pronoun? *its*
　　　　2. What lost *its* petals and comes before *its*? *flower*
　　　　The antecedent of the pronoun *its* is *flower*.

Directions: Find the pronouns and antecedents in these sentences.

|  | Pronouns | Antecedents |
|---|---|---|
| 1. Joe said "My book is gone!" | _____ | _____ |
| 2. Debbie wanted her lunch now. | _____ | _____ |
| 3. Dennis, do you want to leave? | _____ | _____ |
| 4. The car blew its engine. | _____ | _____ |
| 5. The horse likes his new home. | _____ | _____ |
| 6. Although most major league games are played at night, some do take place during the day. | _____ | _____ |
| 7. The Holidays enjoyed themselves at the barbecue yesterday. | _____ | _____ |
| 8. Jorge, did you go to the races last week? | _____ | _____ |
| 9. Booker is the player who fouled out first in the game last night. | _____ | _____ |
| 10. If the girls get here early, we'll take them to dinner. | _____ | _____ |
| 11. Mohammed, are you driving or walking to school today? | _____ | _____ |
| 12. Does Lupe know that he was chosen for the lead in the play? | _____ | _____ |
| 13. Armando and I gave ourselves a rest. | _____ | _____ |

14. Each girl should pack her own suitcase. _____ _____

15. Even though every boy passed the swimming test, none could do the backstroke. _____ _____

Example: One lost his way.

The pronoun is *his*, and the antecedent is *everyone*.
Let's take it one step further. What if the example had a prepositional phrase between the antecedent and the verb?

Example: One (of the boys) lost his way.

Did anything change? No, a prepositional phrase was added. Note that the pronoun did *not* change to *their* because of the plural word *boys*. So, do *not* say "one of the boys lost their way." The pronoun must agree in number with its antecedent, not with the object of the preposition. Which would you choose? Everyone of the cats washed (its, their) paws. Remember: The preposition is *of the cats*. The best thing to do is cross it out so it doesn't get in your way. Now, choose the word the agrees in number with *everyone*. The correct answer is *its*. Singular pronouns go with singular antecedents. Plurals with plurals. These are singular: *each, either, neither, one, everyone, everyone, nobody, anyone, anybody, someone, somebody.*

Directions: Choose the correct pronoun in each sentence. Write it in the blank. (Hint — Cross out the prepositional phrases.)

1. Neither of the cars had (its, their) tires changed. _____

2. Any one of the players could have bought (his, their) own uniform. _____

3. Does anybody in this class have (his, their) book today? _____

4. Everyone at the game rose to (his, their) feet. _____

5. Each of the cheerleaders has (her, their) own unique personality. _____

6. Does either of the schools put on (its, their) own play? _____

7. One of those six women must have a computer in (her, their) office. _____

8. Does nobody in here care about (his, their) grade? _____

9. Has somebody in this room ever had (his, their) own car? _____

10. Does someone among you students have (his, their) radio on? _____

11. Everybody at school has (his, their) own locker. _____

Let's take a look at plural pronouns now. These are plural pronouns: *several, few, both, many.*

Example: *Several* of the girls had brought *their* own skis.

The pronoun is *their*. Drop out the prepositional phrase, Whose own skis? Don't say *girls*. Remember, *girls* is part of a prepositional phrase. The antecedent of *their* is *several*. A plural pronoun has a plural antecedent.

Directions: In the blanks, write the correct pronoun and the antecedent to which it refers.

**Pronoun**          **Antecedent**

_____    _____   1. One of the books has a funny title on (its, their) cover.

_____    _____   2. No one has (his or her, their) combination memorized.

_____    _____   3. Each is responsible for (her, their) own area in the girl's locker room.

_____    _____   4. Several of the firefighters got smoke in (his, their) lungs.

_____    _____   5. Students and teachers alike enjoy (his or her, their) long lunch periods.

_____    _____   6. Several of the students did not eat (his or her, their) lunch in the cafeteria.

_____    _____   7. Either Jimmy or Bobby will bring (his, their) model train to school.

_____    _____   8. Has anyone in this classroom turned in (his or her, their) homework?

_____    _____   9. Neither Kristine nor Stefanie wants to spend (her, their) free time in a gift shop.

_____    _____   10. Both of the accused demanded (his, their) rights.

_____    _____   11. If anyone wants to do extra work, (he or she, they) needs to see the teacher.

_____    _____   12. You can tell a lot about a person by (his, their) first impression on you.

_____    _____   13. If a student is confused by pronoun-antecedent agreement, (he, or she, they) should see the teacher.

_____    _____   14. Nobody is to turn in (his or her, their) work late.

Directions: In the following exercise, write the correct pronoun in the blank, then draw an arrow from that pronoun *back* to its antecedent.

Example: The bird in the trees has lost one of *its* feathers.

1. Nobody is to bring _____ radio to school.

2. Ernestine and Gabriela seem to have forgotten _____ lines.

3. Neither Mark nor Aaron has any of _____ money left from the trip.

4. Did someone leave _____ watch in the coaches' office?

5. Either Mae or Yvonne will make _____ specialty for the picnic.

6. A person must live up to _____ expectations.

7. Horses and cows have _____ own distinct personalities.

8. Each of the girls needs to tell _____ own version of what happened.

9. Both people wanted _____ own private bathrooms.

10. Not one of the 1400 students in this school has to buy _____ own books.

11. Somebody left _____ picture of Elvis Presley in the main office.

12. Almost everybody has to memorize _____ social security number.

# 4 Subject-Verb Agreement

Like pronouns and antecedents, subjects and their verbs must agree in number. Here's what that means:

Examples: She does the work.
He does work.
They do the work.

When the subject is singular (*she* or *he*), the verb is singular, too (*does*). When the subject is plural (*they*), the verb is plural, too (*do*).

In the present tense, singular verbs end in *s*. *Does* ends in *s*. *Runs*, *jumps*, and *walks* all end in *s*. If your subject is singular, your verb must be singular.

Examples: *Sarah* (singular) *pays* (singular) her little sister to babysit.
*She* (singular) *likes* (singular) to go out on Tuesday nights.

Directions: Circle the correct verb in each sentence.

1. She (is, are) the smartest person in school.

2. Tom (want, wants) to take karate lessons.

3. The captain (shout, shouts) commands from the bridge.

4. He (signal, signals) toward the boat.

5. The car (run, runs) on unleaded gas.

There are two exceptions: I and you. Always treat these two pronouns as though they are plural, and don't use present tense verbs that end in *s* with them.

Examples: He does work.
I do the work.
You do the work.

Some people but have trouble making subjects and vebs agree in the negative. If it's "He does," then it's also "He doesn't."

Directions: Circle the correct verb in each sentence.

1. You (depend, depends) on your parents for food and shelter.

2. I (say, says) that you can't swim across the lake.

3. Each (has, have) his own boat for the race.

4. Someone (dive, dives) off the roof of the patio boat.

5. The lake (rise, rises) each winter.

6. Neither (ski, skis) as well as Shannon.

7. She (don't, doesn't) want to fish with worms.

8. The children (dream, dreams) of swimming in the pool.

9. The birds (build, builds) nests in the trees around Shasta Lake.

10. Somebody (give, gives) a sermon every Sunday.

11. None (is, are) correctly priced.

# Agreement and Prepositional Phrases

Sometimes a prepositional phrase comes between the subject and verb. When this happens some people have trouble with subject-verb agreement. The verb must always agree with the subject.

Examples: None of the bikes (is, are) red.
Neither of the boxes (is, are) big enough.

Since *bikes* and *boxes* are both part of prepositional phrases, they cannot be subjects and do not have to agree in number with the verbs. Then, what are the subjects to those two sentences? *None* and *neither* are the subjects. The prepositional phrases do not affect this. When you're determining subject-verb agreement in a sentence that contains a prepositional phrase, cross out the prepositional phrase, and then deal with subject-verb agreement.

Example: Each of the fish (has, have) blue gills.

Cross out *of the fish*. Now, would you say, "Each has blue gills" of "Each have blue gills"? *Each has*, of course. The singular subject requires a singular verb.

Directions: Circle the correct verb.

1. None of the participants (find, finds) the game exciting.

2. One of the house guests (leave, leaves) his key under the mat.

3. All (take, takes) pride in their work.

4. All of the children (reach, reaches) their potential at our school.

5. Someone (open, opens) the gate everyday.

6. Neither of the two girls (has, have) her homework completed.

7. I (stay, stays) very close to the house on weekends.

8. Everyone of the students (know, knows) what the assignment is.

9. In this class anybody (do, does) well who wants to.

10. Sarah and Ruthie (live, lives) down the street.

11. Either of the dresses (look, looks) good on her.

12. Both (was, were) good quarterbacks.

13. Both Gloria and Phyllis (share, shares) the same problem.

14. Most (do, does) their work in auto shop.

15. Most of the members (is, are) avid skiers.

16. Few (seek, seeks) enjoyment at the arcade.

17. Few of the teenagers in Northbrook (play, plays) in a band.

18. Several (need, needs) a place to live.

19. Several of the girls (dive, dives) into the deep end of the pool.

20. Nobody in this large group of men (fear, fears) grizzly bears.

21. You (was, were) the first to sign the petition.

22. Each of the runners (change, changes) lanes too soon.

23. Another of the skiers (teach, teaches) at Alpine Meadows.

24. Any one of the firefighters (put, puts) out both large and small blazes.

25. No one in this school (drink, drinks) the new softdrink.


# Either and Neither

*Either* and *neither* are singular. Don't be confused when another word accompanies them. They require singular verbs.

    Example: Either Dave or John *makes* (singular) his own kites.
                Neither Susie nor Debbie *wants* (singular) to go to the lake.

To find the subject, cross out the words with *either* and *neither*. In the cases above, cross out "Dave or John" and "Susie nor Debbie."

Directions: For each sentence, circle the correct verb.

1. Neither the car nor the truck (run, runs) very well.

2. Either the Eagles or the Warriors (play, plays) this Thursday.

3. Either Jimmy or Edward (work, works) for the city of Chicago.

4. Neither the mail carrier nor the milk deliverer (come, comes) in the morning.

5. Either Shannon or Heather (has, have) a part in the play.

When a sentence begins with *there* or *here*, do not identify either of these as the subject.

    Example: There are two days of school left.

In this case, the subject follows the verb. The verb is *are*. Who or what *are left*? *Days* are left. Remember, *of school* is a prepositional phrase and cannot be the subject.

Directions: Circle the subject in each sentence.

1. There are five pieces of paper on the floor.

2. Here is the report on the dam.

3. There is no one in that room.

4. Here are ten questions for you to answer.

5. There is my pen on the table.

Let's take this one step further. No matter where the subject is located in the sentence, it must agree in number with the verb.

Example: Here (is, are) the books that you requested.

Remember, *here* cannot be the subject. The subject is *books*. *Books* must agree in number with the verb. A plural subject needs a plural verb. *Are* is the plural verb.

Don't make a contraction mistake, by saying something like, "Here's the books." *Here's* means *here is*.

Directions: Circle the correct words in the sentences below.

1. There (is, are) all of my keys on the kitchen counter.

2. (Here's, Here are) several of my report cards from grade school.

3. (There's, There are) one of my best friends.

4. Here (is, are) someone who can write his name correctly.

5. (Here's, Here are) the workers now from the water department.

There are some nouns that end in *s* but are singular. They are called collective nouns. They take a singular verb. Here is a list of some common collective nouns: *mathematics, news, athletics, politics, pair, measles, mumps, dollars.*

Example: Mathematics *is* my favorite subject.

Directions: Circle the correct words.

1. Everybody (has, have) studied for the test.

2. It (don't, doesn't) seem to be too hard.

3. The lady with all the buttons (is, are) the president.

4. None of the snow (was, were) removed last night.

5. The news about the war (is, are) bad.

6. Either the train or the bus (is, are) the cheapest way to travel.

7. Neither the hotel nor the restaurant (take, takes) reservations.

8. None of the women (was, were) going to the convention.

9. Most of the girls (like, likes) the new music.

10. She (don't, doesn't) feel like working on math tonight.

11. (Here's, Here are) the directions to get to my house.

12. (There's, There are) the parts I've been looking for.

13. You (was, were) really moving along fast.

14. So, I (call, calls) her on the phone every night.

15. Athletics (is, are) what keeps me in school.

16. This pair of pants (is, are) ripped.

17. One hundred dollars (is, are) a lot of money.

18. Both the plumber and the electrician (charge, charges) a great deal for their work.

19. Several of the players (take, takes) vitamins.

20. Mom with her club (go, goes) on a trip each month.

21. Politics (is, are) a subject that he'll argue any time.

22. Neither of the buses (leave, leaves) early.

23. Mumps (is, are) a childhood disease.

24. There (is, are) many students in school this year.

25. One of the problems (is, are) incorrectly written.

# Correct Verb Usage

1. Has the tardy bell (rang, rung) yet?

2. I should've (ate, eaten) in the cafeteria.

3. We (laid, lay) out at the lake.

4. You should've (went, gone) to the mall with us.

5. He (drunk, drank) the whole can of soda.

6. He'd (fell, fallen) off that step before.

7. They should've (sang, sung) longer.

8. I (seen, saw) him at lunch in the hallway.

9. I could've (wrote, written) more.

10. I (busted, broke) my pencil.

Did you have trouble choosing the correct verb for each sentence? To choose the correct verb, you need to choose the correct tense. *Tense* means *time*. We will review the present, past, and past participle (used after *have, has* and *had*). The past participle usually shows action has been completed.

> Example: verb — freeze
>> Present tense: Right now, I *freeze* when I'm in snow.
>> Past tense: I *froze* all winter when we lived in Tahoe years ago.

Past with *have, has, had* or past participle: She *has frozen* in the snow, even wearing a parka.

Directions: Look at the list on this page. Then do the exercises that follow, referring to this list as necessary. With practice, correct verb usage will become automatic. Just remember, use a past participle with *have, has,* or *had.*

| Present | Past | Past Participle |
|---|---|---|
| begin | began | (have, has, or had) begun |
| break | broke | (have, has, or had) broken |
| bring | brought | (have, has, or had) brought |
| burst (never bust) | burst | (have, has, or had) burst |
| buy | bought | (have, has, or had) bought |
| choose | chose | (have, has, or had) chosen |
| climb | climbed | (have, has, or had) climbed |
| come | came | (have, has, or had) come |
| do | did | (have, has, or had) done |
| drink | drank | (have, has, or had) drunk |
| drive | drove | (have, has, or had) driven |

| | | |
|---|---|---|
| drown | drowned | (have, has, or had) drowned |
| eat | ate | (have, has, or had) eaten |
| fall | fell | (have, has, or had) fallen |
| freeze | froze | (have, has, or had) frozen |
| give | gave | (have, has, or had) given |
| go | went | (have, has, or had) gone |
| grow | grew | (have, has, or had) grown |
| know | knew | (have, has, or had) known |
| lay | laid | (have, has, or had) laid |
| leave | left | (have, has, or had) left |
| lie | lay | (have, has, or had) lain |
| ride | rode | (have, has, or had) ridden |
| ring | rang | (have, has, or had) rung |
| run | ran | (have, has, or had) run |
| see | saw | (have, has, or had) seen |
| set | set | (have, has, or had) set |
| shrink | shrank | (have, has, or had) shrunk |
| sing | sang | (have, has, or had) sung |
| sink | sank | (have, has, or had) sunk |
| speak | spoke | (have, has, or had) spoken |
| swim | swam | (have, has, or had) swum |
| take | took | (have, has, or had) taken |
| tear | tore | (have, has, or had) torn |
| throw | threw | (have, has, or had) thrown |
| write | wrote | (have, has, or had) written |
| sit | sat | (have, has, or had) sat |
| raise | raised | (have, has, or had) raised |
| rise | rose | (have, has, or had) risen |
| beat | beat | (have, has, or had) beaten |

Directions: Circle the correct verb. Remember to watch for *have*, *has*, or *had*.

1. I have (began, begun) to rock climb.

2. She has (broke, broken) her pick.

3. He has (brung, brought) his climber's chalk.

4. The rock had (busted, burst) open at the point of stress.

5. He (buyed, bought) good climbing boots.

6. He had (chose, chosen) the correct knot for his rope.

7. They thought that they had (clumb, climbed) to the top of the rock.

8. We had (came, come) halfway up the mountain before we rested.

9. She should have (did, done) better on her first climb.

10. The climber (drank, drunk) a lot of water after the climb.

11. The lead climber has (drove, driven) his pick into the rock.

12. Had he fallen off the rock and into the lake, he would have (drowned, drowned).

13. Erosion had (ate, eaten) the rock away.

14. When the lead climber slipped, the whole group had (fell fallen) back a step.

15. His hand had (froze, frozen) firmly when he lost his footing.

16. The sheer face of the rock had (gave, given) them a real challenge.

17. She had (went, gone) up this rock many times.

18. The climb (grew, growed) more difficult with each step.

19. Good climbing is something that he had (knew, known) for a long time.

20. The environment had been (leaved, left) clean by using the new climbing pieces.

Directions: Select the correct form of the verb and write it in the blank.

ride     1. She has _____ that horse many times.

ring     2. The bell _____ long before she was in her seat.

run     3. They have _____ the track.

see     4. When he climbed the mountain, he _____ the ocean.

shrink     5. The shirt has _____ two inches in the sleeves.

sing     6. The choir _____ the national anthem.

sink     7. A large ship had _____ off the coast of San Pedro.

speak     8. The guest had _____ about the importance of staying fit.

swim     9. She had _____ four laps before she quit.

take     10. The boy had _____ the whole period to finish the test.

tear     11. The woman had _____ the letter in two.

throw     12. The cook _____ the pizza dough into the air.

write     13. His mother had _____ an excuse for his absence.

beat     14. The Bulldogs have _____ the Huskies for the first time.

burst     15. An antique bottle _____ as it hit the floor.

drink     16. I _____ four glasses of water daily.

eat     18. Has she _____ at the new restaurant?

go     19. I wish that you had _____ with us.

ride     20. Nobody doubted that he had _____ the full twenty miles.

swim     21. Everybody _____ across the lake before summer had ended.

choose     22. She has _____ to take college prep courses.

# Lie and Lay

Six words that cause trouble in choosing the correct verb are *lie*, *lay*, *rise*, *raise*, *sit*, and *set*.
Let's start with *lie* and *lay*.

       *lay* — to put down      *lie* — to rest

Before you can *lay* something down, you must first pick it up. *Lay* always takes a direct object. Can you *lay* (yourself) down to take a nap? Can you pick yourself up? Try it! You can't. So, if you can't pick yourself up, then you can't *lay* yourself down. So never day. "I want to lay down."

Pick up your pen or pencil. *Lay* it down. Pick up a piece of paper. *Lay* it down. Pick up your book. *Lay* it down. Anything you can pick up, you can *lay* down. *Lying (lie)* down must be done under your own power. Nothing else is involved.

Examples: A dog can *lie* down.

You can *lie* out in the sun.
A flower can *lie* in a planter.
A snake can *lie* on a rock.
A towel can *lie* on the floor.

If somebody or something picks up the dog, you, the flower, the snake, or the towel, then *they* can *lay* them down.

Directions: Fill in the blanks with *lie* or *lay*.

1. He picked up the box, and now he is going to _____ it down.

2. The cat likes to _____ on the rug.

3. The horse wants to _____ in the pasture.

4. Now that you've taken the clothes off the line, you can _____ them on the bed.

5. She needs to _____ down for a short rest.

6. Pick up the book and _____ it on my desk.

7. I like to _____ out by my pool.

8. _____ down by the fire.

9. He wanted to _____ all his clothes on the floor of his room.

10. She told her dog to _____ down.

Like all verbs, *lie* and *lay* have tenses, and that's where most people become confused. Take a look and compare *lie* and *lay* in each tense. The present participle refers to action going on as the same time as other action.

| Present | Past | Past Participle | Present Participle |
|---------|------|-----------------|--------------------|
| lie | lay | lain | lying |
| lay | laid | laid | laying |

Look at the past tense of *lie*. Do you see why it's so confusing? The past tense of *lie* is the present tense of *lay*. However, once again, remember that if you're going to use any tense of *lay* (to put), you must first have picked something up. So, always ask yourself, "Has anything been picked up?" If yes, then you want *lay*. If not, you want *lie*. Then determine *when* the action in the sentence takes place and choose the tense of the correct verb.

Examples: Yesterday, I (lay, laid) on the sofa all day.
Step 1 — Was anything picked up? No. So you want *lie*.
Step 2 — When did the action take place? Yesterday or in the past.
Step 3 — Past tense of *lie* is *lay*; so the correct answer above is *lay*.

Examples: He has (lain, laid) his fishing pole on the bank of the river.
Step 1 — Was anything picked up? Yes, a fishing pole. So you want *lay*.
Step 2 — When did the action take place? In the past plus *has*, so use the past participle.
Step 3 — Past participle of *lay* is *laid*; so the correct answer above is *laid*.

Examples: The dog is (lying, laying) on the porch.
Step 1 — Was anything picked up? No. So you want *lie*.
Step 2 — When did the action take place? Now or in the present plus *is*, so use the present participle.
Step 3 — Present participle of *lie* is *lying*, so the answer above is *lying*.

Directions: Apply the same three-step method to the following sentences. Circle the correct answer.

1. That book has (lain, laid) there for a week.

2. The ball is (lying, laying) right on the forty-yard line.

3. She is (lying, laying) the plates on the table.

4. The hog loves to (lie, lay) in the mud.

5. Earlier this morning I (lay, laid) on the beach at Hermosa.

6. That car had (lain, laid) in the ditch for three days.

7. (Lie, Lay) your pencils here when you're finished.

8. The crew has (lain, laid) three miles of pipe already.

9. Last night, as I (lay, laid) in bed, I worried about the test.

10. Your wallet is (lying, laying) on the floor.

11. They are (lying, laying) their helmets on the bench.

12. A bird is (lying, laying) in its nest.

13. She knew that she had (lain, laid) the dollar on her dresser.

14. The note is (lying, laying) by the refrigerator.

15. I want to (lie, lay) on the white sands of Hawaii.

16. She had to (lie, lay) her gloves down in the ski lodge.

17. A snake (lay, laid) in the path since early morning.

18. They had (lain, laid) the bases on the field.

19. The horses have (lain, laid) in the shade during the heat wave.

20. Smog is (lying, laying) over the Los Angeles basin.

# Rise and Raise

There's a simple solution to choosing between *rise* and *raise*. Something must be *raised* by an outside force. On the other hand, something *rises* under its own power. Something must be picked up to be *raised*.

Examples: He *raised* the flag over the courthouse.

You can pick up the flag, so you can raise it.

Examples: He *raised* up to his feet.

You cannot literally pick up yourself, so you cannot raise yourself.

Can you pick up a football? Of course! Then you can raise it over your head. Can you pick up your hand? Of course! Then you can raise it over your head. Can you pick up the telephone receiver? Of course! Then you can raise it over you head.

Directions: In the blanks below, name ten items that you can pick up and raise over your head.

1. _____     6. _____
2. _____     7. _____
3. _____     8. _____
4. _____     9. _____
5. _____     10. _____

On the other hand, something *rises* by its own force. If something *rises*, it's doing it under its own power. Smoke *rises*. Heat *rises*. The temperature *rises*. A sleeping cat *rises*. A ghost *rises* out of the tomb.

Directions: In the blanks below, name ten items that *rise* under their own power.

1. _____     6. _____
2. _____     7. _____
3. _____     8. _____
4. _____     9. _____
5. _____     10. _____

Here are the tenses of *raise* and *rise*:

| Present | Past | Past Participle | Present Participle |
|---------|------|-----------------|--------------------|
| raise | raised | raised | raising |
| rise | rose | risen | rising |

In the following examples, note that the something that can be picked up and *raised* is in italics. The verb rise or raise is printed in bold type. If the action is caused by the subject's own force, then, of course, it's *rising* and nothing will be in italics.

Examples:
1. The soldiers **raised** the *cannon* to a higher position.
2. The outlaw, Tom Horn, **rose** from his bunk early in the morning.
3. She **raises** her *eyebrows* when she's joking.
4. The sun is **rising** earlier each day.
5. The humidity **has risen** steadily since it's been cloudy.
6. Why does he keep **raising** that *card* over his head?
7. They went to town to **raise** *heck* and have a good time.
8. On the hilltop, they have **raised** a *monument* to the fallen heroes.
9. Echoing through the tops of the fir trees, the sound of the raging fire **rose to a** frightening roar.
10. This new evidence **has raised** *doubts* about his guilt.

Directions: Supply the missing words.

1. Because of their generosity, the town _____ enough money to help the boy with the needed operation.

2. He wants to _____ his standing in the community.

3. Your last statement has _____ still another operation.

4. Angered, the father slowly _____ from his chair.

5. Since the new governor took office, the economy has _____ dramatically.

6. Only you have the ability to _____ your grade.

7. The team is _____ the coach onto the victory platform.

8. Her fears are _____ about the upcoming election.

9. With a clang of the cymbals, the crescendo of the music begins to _____

10. The hills _____ gradually from the valley floor.

Directions: Fill in the blanks with the proper tense of *raise* or *rise*.

1. When I'm camping on Shasta Lake, I usually _____ early enough to fish before the sun comes up.

2. One time I _____ at 4:30 A.M. and had to wait an hour to see enough to bait my hook.

3. My grandfather said that he has _____ as early as 2.00 A.M. to fish on the ocean.

4. When I fish I try not to _____ a commotion and scare the fish.

5. Generally, I use a fly to try to make the fish _____ to the surface of the water.

6. I have _____ some of the toughest fighters in the lake on some of the simplest flies.

7. People say that if the lake keeps _____, fishing will be even better.

8. Yesterday, I _____ a large German brown that went after a yellow nymph.

9. I understand that they are _____ the level of the lake one foot a day.

10. Tomorrow, I will _____ at 5:00 A.M. to try to work the "morning bite."

Directions: Circle the correct verb.

1. I want to (rise, raise) a steer for 4-H.

2. Dad likes to (lie, lay) on the sofa and watch baseball on TV.

3. I have been (lying, laying) in bed all day with a cold.

4. She has (rose, raised) over four hundred dollars for the scouts.

5. A misty haze has (risen, raised) over the valley.

6. That cat has (lain, laid) in front of the door for three days.

7. Yesterday, it (lay, laid) there until I fed it.

8. My opinion of you has (risen, raised).

9. She has (risen, raised) the price in her store.

10. I have (lain, laid) the documents in front of you.

11. Through the tunnel, the crew (lay, laid) the tracks for the train.

12. The Hudson River is (rising, raising) with the heavy rainfall.

13. The heavy rainfall is (rising, raising) the lever of the river.

14. He walked over to the window and (rose, raised) the shade.

15. Now that he has picked up that heavy bar bell, he must (lie, lay) it down somewhere.

16. She has (lain, laid) out her plans for the new house.

17. The city is (lying, laying) out its proposal for another bridge over the river.

18. The odor of that garbage is likely to (rise, raise) and make the tenants of the apartments unhappy.

19. The plane (rose, raised) up through the clouds and flew off toward Fantasy Island.

20. I'm used to (lying, laying) on my back when I sleep.

21. These ruins have (lain, laid) there for thousands of years.

# Sit and Set

Now we've come to the last two troublesome verbs, *sit* and *set*. To sit means to put yourself into a seated position. To set means to place something down or to put into place Notice that word *something*. You're dealing with another object when you use *set* as you did with *lay* and *raise*. Also, as with *lie* and *rise*, you *sit* under your own power.

Examples: 1. Please pick up that book, then *set* it down.
2. Please come over here and *sit* in this chair.

| Present | Past | Present Participle | Present Participle |
|---------|------|-------------------|-------------------|
| sit | sat | sat | sitting |
| set | set | set | setting |

Notice anything peculiar about *set* in the first three tenses? It's the same in all three tenses. Even in the present participle, it is the same only with -*ting* added. When you use *set*, you must have some *thing* to put or place. You can *set* a goal. You can *set* a package down. You can *set* your watch. You can *set* the table. You can *set* a course of action. When you *sit*, you do this under your own power.

Directions: Circle the correct verb.

1. We had to (sit, set) in the front row.

2. We (sat, set) the boxes in the hallway.

3. We (sat, set) there on the sofa for three hours.

4. She is (sitting, setting) silverware on the table.

5. They are (sitting, setting) in our places.

Directions: Decide which word is correct and write it in the blank.

1. The bottle is _____ on the shelf.

2. She has _____ in the first desk for three months now.

3. Do you want to _____ any place special to watch this movie?

4. His grandmother said, "Come on in and _____ down so we can talk."

5. Is she _____ the table for the banquet?

6. They _____ on their tails all day and did nothing.

7. Who is that boy _____ over by the window?

8. Should he _____ an extra place for our company?

9. Where has he _____ the new stereo?

10. He _____ the old stereo in his sister's bedroom.

11. I wish she would _____ by me on the bus.

12. The only thing she _____ by me on the bus was her books.

13. I am _____ this here for all of you to look at.

14. Do you like to _____ on the patio in the afternoon?

15. We _____ anywhere that we wanted last year in English.

16. He is _____ a new goal for himself in school.

17. Last week, they _____ sail for Hawaii.

18. The manager said that they have _____ their prices as low as they possibly could on the new cars.

19. The dog _____ happily wagging his tail.

20. He said that they had _____ under that same tree when they were young.

Directions: If you think the verb (lie, lay, rise, raise, sit, set) is used correctly, put a C in the blank. If it's used incorrectly, put an I in the blank.

Example: ___I___    1. Jane is setting on the chair.

___C___    2. Lay your hand on the book and swear to tell the whole truth and nothing but the truth.

_____    1. They were setting up the podium for the assembly.

_____    2. On the beach, you could see the people laying in the sun.

_____    3. Her expectations are raising about the new year.

_____    4. Steam was rising from the hot coffee.

_____    5. He tried to raise his hand over his head after the operation.

_____    6. They have set in the family room all day just watching TV.

_____    7. Sitting on a rock, the lizard flicked its tongue continuously.

_____    8. The star began to raise and peek over the top of the mountain.

_____    9. Lying on the ground, the coin obviously had been lost for years.

_____    10. Grandpa had laid in bed with his illness for three years.

_____  11. She set her belongings on the chair as she entered the room.

_____  12. The clouds had risen rapidly up the slopes of the mountain.

_____  13. Ask your mother if you can go to the country and lay out under the pines and listen to my stereo.

_____  14. I lay there for a while, listening to the sounds of the train roaring through the windy river canyon.

_____  15. The city of Philadelphia is raising the price of their electricity again.

_____  16. My dad says that they should set a standard rate for everybody.

_____  17. He is laying new ground rules for me to follow when I go on dates.

_____  18. She is lying the towels in the wrong place.

_____  19. The pterodactyl raised up in flight over the frightened boy scout troop below.

_____  20. The boy scout troop rose in anger as it saw the pterodactyl descend from its nest.

_____  21. Prices have raised continuously since 1965.

_____  22. I'd like to set your mind straight on that matter.

_____  23. Does a ptarmigan lie eggs?

_____  24. The robin outside my window is trying to rise a worm from the garden.

_____  25. He has set in the vice principal's office all year.

_____  26. He says that he wants his reputation to raise so that people will respect him.

_____  27. The vice principal raised up out of her seat when she saw the boy entered her office for the third time in a week.

_____  28. The noise of the shot had rose over the sound of the voices.

_____  29. A crocodile laid under the shady bush.

_____  30. They have raised their standards for admission at the University of Iowa.

_____  31. If you want to set by me, you'll have to be quiet.

_____  32. You need to set a good example for your little brother.

_____  33. If you know the answer to this question, raise your hand.

_____  34. Lay your guitar down and stop screaming into the microphone.

_____  35. We need to rise $400 by December 1.

_____  36. His grades have been raising since he moved from the city.

_____  37. The town of Round Mountain is a good place to raise kids.

_____  38. Laying on the sidewalk was a dollar bill.

_____  39. The cricket laid there for a while without making a noise.

_____  40. Lay on your stomach if you have indigestion.

_____  41. Those precious gems have laid in the pyramids for thousands of years.

_____ 42. She laid all her hopes and dreams on a good education.

_____ 43. We have lain our proposal out to you in detail.

_____ 44. In just two weeks, the Union Pacific Railroad had laid a thousand miles of track.

_____ 45. The hummingbird has raised its head to drink from the feeder.

_____ 46. We had rose a flag to signal the start of the race.

_____ 47. We set right by the orchestra.

_____ 48. They set over by the wall.

_____ 49. The pilot sat the plane down very gently.

_____ 50. Mr. Skelly has set the stuffed armadillo on the front table so that everybody can see it.

Directions: Use the tense of the verb indicated to write a sentence. Also, circle the verb that you've used.

Example: go (past participle) Because of the enormous amount of support of the fans in Chicago, the Cubs have gone to the World Series. Refer to the list on page ____ for help on this exercise.

1. lie (past) _____

_____

2. drink (past participle) _____

_____

3. swim (past participle) _____

_____

4. sit (present) _____

_____

5. throw (past) _____

_____

6. knew (past) _____

_____

7. shrink (past) _____

_____

8. ring (past participle) _____

_____

9. rise (present) _____

_____

10. ride (past participle) _____

_____

11. set (present) _____

_____

12. see (past participle) _____

_____

# 6

# Clauses

A clause is a group of words with both a subject and a verb that is used as part of a sentence. Some clauses are dependent, which means they cannot be a sentence alone. Other clauses are independent, which means that they can be a sentence alone. Clauses can be used as certain parts of speech. There are adverb clauses, adjective clauses, and noun clauses. We will study adverb clauses first.

## Adverb Clauses

Before we begin on adverb clauses, let's review the basics about adverbs. An adverb describes verbs, adjectives, and other adverbs. It answers the questions: *when, where, how, why,* and *to what extent.*

So far you've studied adverbs as single words such as *slowly, rapidly, quickly, quietly, very, too,* and *high.* An adverb can also be a group of words. That's what a clause is — a group of words that has a subject and a verb. The following are clauses. Though they are not complete sentences, they are still clauses because they contain both subject and verb.

1. If she needs help
2. When the team runs off the field
3. After the class is dismissed

These clauses above are known as "dependent" clauses because they are dependent on another clause for their completion. In other words, they cannot stand alone. They must be attached to another clause that can stand alone (an independent clause). Note the examples of independent clauses below.

Examples: 1. You can show her how to ski better.
2. The crowd always cheers.
3. The teacher usually straightens up the room.

What's the difference between these clauses and the dependent clauses? Don't these seem to express a complete thought or idea? They can stand alone. They don't need to be attached to anything to make sense. They are, indeed, independent. Let's attach the dependent clauses above to the independent clauses above, and you'll probably recognize which is dependent upon the other for completion.

Examples: 1. If she needs help, you can show her how to ski better.
2. When the team runs off the field, the crowd always cheers.
3. After the class is dismissed, the teacher usually straightens up the room.

Directions: In the exercise below, underline the dependent clause once and the independent clause twice.

1. When he finally saw his score, he was a little surprised.

2. After the game was over, Joanna was totally exhausted.

3. If you can show me a 1957 Chevrolet in mint condition, I'll buy it.

4. Because we're running late today, I'll have to give you this assignment as homework.

5. While she waited for the bus, Beverly did her homework.

6. Until he was an adult, Jamaal had never seen a live horse.

7. Unless they hurry, they'll never finish the race before dark.

8. Although she wanted to go to the prom in a Mercedes, she settled for Pedro's old truck.

Not all dependent clauses come at the beginning of the sentence. They can also follow an independent clause or fall in the middle of an independent clause. In these examples, the independent clause is underlined twice and the dependent clause is underlined once.

Examples: He read a great book that was assigned in his history class.

She cleaned her entire apartment after the party was over.

That house that was built in 1851 is a California historical site.

The person who invented the microchip is an absolute genius.

Directions: In the exercise below, underline the dependent clause once and the independent clause twice.

1. The medical collateral ligament that is the most commonly injured is the one on the inside of your knee.

2. He gets a lot of great exercise when he rides his bicycle.

3. She didn't know the reason for the accident until she read the report.

4. Even though my third period class is on the other side of the campus, I can usually make it on time.

5. The victim whomever he may be should always be covered to prevent exposure.

6. She wants to go the Air Force Academy if she can keep her grades up.

7. He bought a great racing horse that was the son of Midnight Magic.

8. As soon as the race was over, the crowd rushed toward Althea.

9. She didn't know how well off she was until she visited South America.

10. The moon which is our only natural satellite orbits the earth.

An adverb clause, then, is a group of words that is used as an adverb and answer *where, when, why, how* or *to what extent.*

Let's look at the adverb question: *when* and an example clause — *after he opens the gifts.* Because the clause answers the question *when*, it is an adverb clause. An adverb clause does what adverbs do. It answers the same questions that single-word adverbs do.

Adverb clauses are attached to independent clauses.

Example: *After he opens the gifts, we'll have cake and ice cream.*

| fragment | not a fragment |
|---|---|
| dependent clause | independent clause |
| can't be by itself | can be by itself |

Directions: Fill in the blank with an independent clause that goes with this adverb clause.

1. Because he knew the teacher would find out, _____

_____

Directions: Attach his adverb clause to an independent clause.

2. _____ as soon as your father gets home.

Notice that an adverb clause, like a single word adverb, can move around. It can be at the beginning of the sentence or at the end of the sentence. You could reverse the position of these clauses and the sentence would still maintain the same meaning. Try it.

Directions: Now pick out the adverb clause and underline it.

3. He liked to run because it kept his body and mind healthy.

Did you choose *because it kept his body and mind healthy?* Great! Which adverb question does this clause

answer? _____

Directions: Write five sentences, three of them beginning with adverb clauses and two ending with adverb clauses. The adverb clauses you use must answer the questions listed. Underline your adverb clauses.

| why? | 1. _____ |
| when? | 2. _____ |
| to what extent? | 3. _____ |
| when? | 4. _____ |
| why? | 5. _____ |

# Adjective Clauses

An adjective describes a noun or pronoun. It answers the questions *what one, which kind,* and *how many.* The question that most adjective clauses answer is *which one.*

Adjectives describe nouns and pronouns. Adjective clauses describe nouns and pronouns. So, when you're identifying adjective clauses, look for a group of words that describes a noun or pronoun. Most of the time adjective clauses will describe nouns. They may describe pronouns. Here's an example of an adjective clause describing a pronoun:

Example: It was she *who scored the highest in the class.*

The adjective clause is *who scored the highest in the class;* it describes she. It tells which she.

Example: This is he *who landed the plane on one wheel.*

Which he is this? The he who landed the plane on one wheel. One word or a group of words that describes a noun or a pronoun is an adjective. The adjective clause here is *who landed the plane on one wheel* and it describes the pronoun *he.*

Let's deal with the rule now instead of the exception. Most adjective clauses describe nouns.

Example: The man is well qualified.

Okay, let's ask that adjective question. Which man is well qualified?
Answer: That I am going to vote for.

That's a clause. It has both subject (I) and verb (am going), but it is a fragment, so it's dependent. It is, indeed, an adjective clause, telling which man. Let's put the two clauses together. The man *that I am going to vote for* is well qualified.

Example: The house *that was sold last week* needs painting.

Which house needs painting? The house *that was sold last week*. In this clause, *that* is the subject and *was sold* is the verb. It can't stand alone, so it's dependent or a fragment. It tells which house (a noun). So, if it answers which and describes a noun, it has to be an adjective. It is, indeed, an adjective clause.

Directions: Write an adjective clause in the blank. (Hint: start with *that*).

The Shakespearean play _____ is *Romeo and Juliet*.

Does what you wrote start with *that*? It probably should. Does what you wrote have a subject and a verb? It must! Can what you wrote stand alone as a complete sentence? It shouldn't be able to if it's a dependent clause.

Directions: Fill in the next set of blanks with adjective clauses.

1. The team _____ is the Houston Oilers.

2. The lady _____ has found it.

3. A subject _____ is geometry.

4. Fargo _____ has close to 50,000 people within the city limits.

5. It was I _____ .

Directions: Let's reverse the process. Write an independent clause to go along with the adjective clause that is supplied for you.

1. _____ that is about 400 miles from Denver _____

_____

2. _____ whom I most admire.

3. _____ that I want to read most _____

_____

4. _____ that is a good place to eat _____

_____

5. _____ who took the last cookie from the jar.

# Noun Clauses

A noun can be a subject, predicate nouns, direct object, indirect object, or object of a preposition. Noun clauses can be subjects, and they can be objects. They can also be predicate nouns. Let's look at some prime examples. First, let's create a dependent clause: whatever she wants. Let's use that clause as a noun by making it the subject of a sentence: *Whatever she wants* is fine with him.

You remember how to find a subject of a sentence. First, find the verb. Then, ask who or what is doing the verb. The answer is the subject. Find the verb in the sentence above. The verb is *is*. Now ask who or what is fine with him. The answer, of course, is the clause *whatever she wants*. The clause is the subject. All subjects must be either a noun or a pronoun. Since this is a clause and it's the subject, it is a noun clause. There's no such thing as a pronoun clause.

Look at another noun clause used as a subject: *Whichever pair fits* is the one to buy. That same group of words above, *whichever pair fits*, can be used in a different way as a noun clause if you put it somewhere else in a sentence. For example, let's put it where you'd normally find a direct object: You should wear *whichever pair fits*. Review direct objects in the complement section of this text-workbook if you need to brush up on them. Here's another noun clause used as a direct object: You can say *whatever comes to your mind*.

Let's use a noun clause as a predicate noun. Predicate nouns rename the subject. It might be a good idea to review that section of this text-workbook if you're the least bit unsure. Once again, let's create a noun clause: that everyone is free of pain. Now let's put *that* where you'd normally find a predicate noun in a sentence. The young physician's *dream was* that everyone is free of pain. *Dream was* — subject and verb. Dream was what? The answer to that question gives you a complement. *Dream and that everyone is free of pain* are the same thing, so this noun clause is a predicate noun.

Can a noun clause be the object of a preposition? Choose the noun clause, *whatever suited him at the time*.

Example: He thought <u>about</u> <u>whatever suited him at the time</u>.

   prep.          object of preposition

Let's use a noun clause as an indirect object. Choose the noun clause — *whoever passes by*.

Example: The man gives *whoever passes by* a pamphlet.

The subject is *man* and the verb is *gives*. What does the man give? A pamphlet. To whom did he give the pamphlet? To *whoever passes by*. It works like an indirect object. That's because this noun clause is an indirect object.

Directions: In the following sentences, tell whether the noun clause (in italics) is a subject, predicate noun, direct object, indirect object, or object of a preposition. You may abbreviate — S, PN, DO, IO, OP.

_____    1. Her wish was *that he return safely to her*.

_____    2. *Whatever you say to me* is not going to make any difference.

_____    3. He said *that you couldn't go*.

_____    4. Bob tells *whoever will listen* his life story.

_____    5. *Whichever one you choose* will fit you nicely.

_____    6. He'll argue about *whatever you want to bring up*.

_____    7. My main concern is *that you drive with care*.

_____    8. She talked about *whoever came into her mind*.

_____    9. Mrs. Redmon knew *that you had not read the chapter*.

Directions: In the blanks to the left, list whether the italicized clauses are adverb clauses, adjective clauses, or noun clauses. Abbreviate them as adv, adj, or n.

Examples: ___adj___    The window *that I broke* is in the back of the house.

          ___n___     *What he said* was very important.

          ___adv___   She didn't know what to think *when he came to the dance with someone else*.

_____    1. He saw immediately *that you were in trouble*.

_____    2. *What he wanted* was to be left alone.

_____

_____

_____

_____

_____

_____

_____

_____

_____

_____

_____

_____

_____

3. The television show *that is my favorite* is "Sesame Street."

4. An American author *whom I greatly admire* is Ray Bradbury.

5. The frightened cat hid under *whatever she could find.*

6. His goal in life was *that he could one day be a ski instructor.*

7. *When he saw the steep hill ahead of him,* he skidded his skis to a stop.

8. That car is the one *that I'm going to buy.* (Think about it. What part of speech is *one?*)

9. She cried *because she had lost the election.*

10. I like anyone *who stands up for his rights.*

11. *Whoever wins this race* will receive a nice prize.

12. He gave *whoever had his hand out* a free ticket.

13. He needed *what they were offering.*

14. The teacher *that everybody likes* is Mr. Moore.

15. *Since everyone did so well on the exercise,* we'll leave early today.

# 7 Punctuation

## End Punctuation

Every sentence must have punctuation at its end. There are three punctuation marks that can be used at the end of a sentence:

Periods end most sentences such as statements, mild commands, and requests.

> Example: Sir Galahad was a skateboard expert. (statement)
> Close the window. (mild command)
> Please take off your hat. (request)

Question marks end direct questions.

> Example: Do you know where you are?

Exclamation marks indicate strong emotion. They are used after single words or complete sentences. (If used too often, exclamation marks lose their effectiveness.)

> Example: Hurray! I got an A.
> Hurray, I got an A!

Directions: Decide which punctuation mark each sentence needs and place it in the space at the end of the sentence.

1. I would like to know when you'll be home ＿＿＿

2. When will you be home ＿＿＿

3. Talk to Juan about it, please ＿＿＿

4. I'll talk to Joe about it ＿＿＿

5. What a day＿＿＿

6. An interrogative sentence asks a question ＿＿＿

7. Is this an interrogative sentence ＿＿＿

8. He asked me if that is true ＿＿＿

9. Ray Bradbury is the author of *The Illustrated Man* ＿＿＿

10. Ow ＿＿＿ I skinned my knee ＿＿＿ (two marks)

11. Did you know that Kennedy High first opened its doors in 1967 ＿＿＿

12. At that time, Jack Schreder was principal ＿＿＿

13. He had high hopes for the ninth grade center ＿＿＿

14. Guess who the vice-principal was ＿＿＿

15. That year 1400 eager freshmen became Kennedy's first class \_\_\_\_

16. The original building was Shasta High School \_\_\_\_

17. Imagine a building built in 1927 still being used today \_\_\_\_

18. Don't you think that Kennedy should be an historical landmark \_\_\_\_

19. What a thrill it would be to see that old building made famous \_\_\_\_

20. Someday all Kennedy's students will have been proud to have attended such a fine school \_\_\_\_

21. The art of fixing eggs is more difficult that one realizes \_\_\_\_

22. Do you know that there are over thirty-seven ways to cook an egg \_\_\_\_

23. You can scramble, poach, boil, or broil them \_\_\_\_

24. How wonderful it is to have such a diverse product \_\_\_\_

25. You can fry them hard, over-easy, or medium \_\_\_\_

26. They can be cooked in casseroles or omelettes \_\_\_\_

27. Can you name other ways to cook an egg \_\_\_\_

28. You can even eat them raw or mix them in orange juice, too \_\_\_\_

29. You can make eggnog and a variety of other drinks \_\_\_\_

30. Eggs are terrific \_\_\_\_

31. Is this class ever long \_\_\_\_

32. It's right before lunch \_\_\_\_

33. Do you know when I ate last \_\_\_\_

34. I ate breakfast this morning \_\_\_\_

35. Did you eat breakfast this morning \_\_\_\_

36. I didn't have time to finish either \_\_\_\_

37. I had to catch the bus \_\_\_\_

38. Boy, am I ever hungry \_\_\_\_

39. Who can think straight when hungry \_\_\_\_

40. I wish this class were over, so I could eat \_\_\_\_

# Commas

If a sentence contains a list of people, things, or ideas, commas are used between the items. For example, in the following sentence, how many people should the police look for?

Example: Jesse James and Bill robbed the bank. Right! Just two. Jesse, James, and Bill robbed the bank. By simply adding a couple of commas, we've suddenly got three suspects. (Important: *don't forget the comma before "and,"*)

Note: Commas aren't needed if all items are joined by *and* or *or:* This example could go on *and* on *and* on.

Directions: First, read each sentence and put commas where they are needed. Then, on the blank lines to the left of the sentences, write the words that *precede* the commas. If the sentence requires no commas, write *no commas* on one of the blanks. I've had shots for measles, mumps, and whooping cough.

Example: ___measles___

___mumps___  I caught chicken pox and jungle fever.

___no commas___

_____  1. The Warrens have a dog two cats and a canary.

_____

_____  2. Get me a pound of butter a loaf of bread and a dozen oranges.

_____

_____  3. Jack dashed into the house grabbed the fire extinguisher and rushed back to the car.

_____

_____  4. Pizza chili fried chicken and apple pie are Robert's favorite foods.

_____

_____

_____  5. Be sure to tell Debbie Rick and Wing where we're bowling tonight.

_____

_____

_____  6. Linus was on first base Peppermint Patty was pitching and Pig Pen was catching.

_____

_____  7. Our club house is old small and drafty.

_____

_____

_____  8. Miss Mullen traveled through Germany or Switzerland or Australia.

_____

_____

_____  9. The department ordered rubber bands paper clips construction paper and chalk.

_____

_____

_____

_____

_____

_____

_____

_____

_____

_____

_____

_____

_____

_____

_____

_____

_____

_____

_____

_____

_____

_____

10. Penny dashed in tossed down her books and ran to the telephone.

11. Do you want steak chops or beef stew for dinner?

12. My neighbor raises chickens cows horses and a terrible odor!

13. She ordered a pair of gloves a silk scarf and a charm bracelet.

14. Miss Wilson advises us to study every day attend all classes and review often.

15. Bring your toothbrush slippers and bathrobe if you plan to stay overnight.

16. After the meeting Alan Jeff Linda and Sam discussed the party.

17. Would you like to go to the movies the bowling alley or the hockey game?

18. He has worked as a cab driver dishwasher brick layer and messenger.

19. My father and my mother and I spent the day at the lake.

20. Ben caught the ball dashed past an end and raced into the end zone.

# Commas in Addresses

When you address an envelope, remember to use one comma, the one between city and state.

Example: Mr. R.U. Thayer
676 Peekaboo Lane
Icyon, Ohio 59427

When the address is in a sentence, separate the items in the address using commas. After the last item, put another comma — unless it's at the end of a sentence, of course. (Note: the word *in* or *at* may make a comma unnecessary.)

Example: Sherlock Holmes supposedly lived on Baker Street, London, England, during the 19th century.

Directions: Put necessary commas in the sentences. Then in the blanks, write each word that precedes a comma. (You may not fill all blanks.)

Example: <u>Ashland</u>      Ashland, Oregon, has a well-known Shakespearean festival.

<u>Oregon</u>

_____

_____      1. The package was sent to Mr. Albert Brown at 941 Parker Drive Denver Colorado.

_____

_____      2. I'm staying at the Hotel Continental 221 Mannix Street San Francisco California for the summer.

_____

_____

_____      3. The address of the Prime Minister of Great Britain is 10 Downing Street London England.

_____

_____      4. Herman lives at the following address:
121 Shaker Avenue
Los Angeles California 96031

_____

_____      5. Laurel was born in Minneapolis Minnesota but grew up in Topeka Kansas.

_____

_____      6. Write to me at 1938 Akron Street Victorville California after October 2.

_____

_____      7. My parents stayed at the Sunrise Motel in Apple Valley Florida.

_____

_____

_____

_____

_____

_____

_____

_____

_____

_____

_____

_____

_____

_____

_____

_____

_____

_____

_____

_____

_____

_____

_____

_____

8. Bob moved from Seattle Washington to Munich Germany.

9. We moved to Sandburg Lane Bangor Maine last summer.

10. Please forward our mail to 924 East Main Street Chicago Illinois 60210 beginning Monday.

11. Betty was born in Dayton Ohio.

12. Dick lived for three years at 300 Coast Street Portland Oregon.

13. During spring vacation they visited relatives in Arlington Virginia and in Washington D.C.

14. He'll spend some time with his brother at 1972 East Third Street Denny California.

15. Brenda sent a Christmas order to Junction Field Chicago Illinois 60210.

16. The Smith family moved from Igo California to 1968 Sandy Way Ono California.

17 Central Valley Pennsylvania is an industrial city.

18. Mail the coupons to the Lambert Company P.O. Box 1775 Clinton Iowa 52735.

_____

_____

_____

_____

19. He asked Mother to pick us up from Marty's 416 Partridge Road.

20. The crew began work at the Blossom Street location in Phoenix.

# Commas in Dates

Write out Friday's date, without using abbreviations. _____

Does your date above look something like this? *February 25, 1988.* If so, you've got the idea about using commas in dates. When you write one in a sentence, just put commas between the main parts of the date and one after the last part. (The last one is often forgotten.)

Example: I left on vacation on Saturday, July 17, 1982, from the San Francisco airport.

Directions: Read each sentence and put in the necessary commas. Then on the blanks to the left, write each word that precedes a comma.

Example:   __Monday__        I was born on Monday, June 21.

_____

_____

_____

_____

_____

_____

_____

_____

_____

_____

_____

_____

_____

_____

1. Margaret's great grandfather was born on Tuesday March 24 1857.

2. In June 1982 the space shuttle was launched from Florida.

3. On Thursday October 24 1929 the stock market crashed.

4. July 4 1776 is an important date in American history.

5. I went to the Rose Bowl Parade on January 1 1980.

# Review

Directions: Insert the correct punctuation in the following sentences.

1. Mary Toni and Jean share an apartment at 107 Carney Road Tallahassee
2. Send your application a resume and references to John Fredricks 916 Oceanside Drive Atlantic City New Jersey 27641
3. Who moved into the place on East Street Denver this month
4. Darn it I thought I'd brought my paper pencil and books to class
5. Seeing the capitol visiting the Railroad Museum and wandering around Old Town are enjoyable activities in Sacramento California

Directions: For extra credit rewrite and punctuate the sentence below. You'll need to put periods after abbreviations like *Ave.*, *a.m.*, or *Mrs.*

1. Mr V Nerschnitzel lives at 1845 E Blossom Blvd Visalia KY 92850

_____

_____

2. Dr Rene Thomas Plans to tour St Moritz Switzerland this summer with Emily Francine and Michele

_____

_____

Directions: Correctly punctuate the following sentences. They need end punctuation and commas in series, addresses, and dates.

1. Jan knew her lines her blocking and her songs for opening night on Thursday May 26
2. Elmont High School 2200 Eureka Way Detroit Michigan 36105 was the address on the envelope
3. In March 1978 did your family move to Mockingbird Lane in Enterprise

Directions: For extra credit rewrite and correctly punctuate the following sentences. Watch for abbreviations requiring periods.

1. I was invited to a reception at Countryside Center 1590 Golflinks Road Fairway Arizona 71668

_____

_____

_____

2. Mom was born on October 7 1943 in Stockton Alabama

_____

_____

_____

3. Between 10 a.m. and 5 p.m. on Wednesday July 27 the circle was set up in a new town

_____

_____

_____

# Commas after an Introduction

In the following sentences notice how one idea runs into another.

    Examples: While we were eating our dog ran from the room.
               No sooner would be better.

To prevent misunderstanding, commas are needed between main ideas and the words that introduce them.

    Examples: No, *sooner would be better.* (*Main idea*)

Certain words used at the beginning of sentences are signals that commas will be needed. If you see the following words starting sentences, be prepared to insert commas at the end of the phrase: *while, when, if, because, although, according to, since, after, before.* Common one-word introductions are *no, yes, oh, well.*

Directions: In the following exercise, place commas after introductory wording. Then on the line to the left, write the word that comes before the comma. Not all sentences require commas. For any sentence needing no comma, write *no comma* on the line.

1. After the game was over John left the stadium.

2. Although she was a good skier she still took lessons.

3. While she was in Colorado she visited Estes Park.

4. Before he skied at Park City he bought new skis.

5. Although the Warriors won the game they were still very humble.

6. If anyone wants a trail map of Shasta Ski Park see Mrs. Hammett.

7. No they lost by three points.

8. In the mountains lies lovely Lassen Park.

9. If you like to ski try Boreal Ridge.

10. Another good place to play tennis is Houston's South City park.

11. When the time came Aaron was ready for the game.

12. After he was out of English Bret threw a party.

13. Since he had passed the English final Barry was ready for advanced composition.

14. Yes all the studying had paid off.

15. Although the worst test was still to come in college Derek seemed ready for anything.

16. While she studied she listened to the radio.

17. Mrs. Spencer is in charge of the counseling center.

_____ 18. According to many students Mr. Hollahan is a real taskmaster.

_____ 19. If you loan me your notes I may pass the test.

_____ 20. Oh please don't stay too long at the club.

Directions: Write five original sentences. Begin each with one of the introductory words that you read about before the last exercise.

1. _____

_____

2. _____

_____

3. _____

_____

4. _____

_____

5. _____

_____

Directions: Correctly punctuate the following sentences using end punctuation and commas in series, addresses, dates, and after introductory wording.

1. We left Boise Idaho on June 24 1975
2. Although I'm on a diet I managed to force down two hotdogs a large soft drink and a triple-decker ice cream cone
3. Well have you finished your homework
4. When Jerry lived at 625 Knights Way Anchorage he attended East Anchorage High School
5. After July 1 1983 you can write to us at 817 Crimson Court Cheyenne Wyoming 85123

Directions: Rewrite the following sentences adding the correct punctuation. Include periods after abbreviations.

1. On January 17 1982 I mailed the unwanted merchandise to PO Box 88 Charlottesville SC for a refund.

_____

_____

2. Before you fold spindle or mutilate me listen to my side of the story.

_____

_____

# Commas with Appositives

Appositives help make something clearer. An appositive is a word or group of words that repeats the meaning of the preceding word or group of words. Because the appositive "interrupts" the sentence, it is set off with commas.

Examples: Terry, *one of our best athletes*, won the race at Red Bluff.
The flags were red and gold, *our school colors.*

Directions: First, read each sentence and underline the appositive. Second, put a comma before the appositive and after it, if necessary. Finally, write the word or words that precede the commas on the lines to the left.

Example:  ___sister___    My sister, the president of the club, wants to have a meeting next
         ___club___    week

_____    1. Skiing John's favorite sport takes a lot of ability.

_____    2. Millions of people men and women enjoy the sport of
_____        skiing.

_____    3. Many people probably thousands flock to a single resort
_____        every weekend.

_____    4. Aspen Heights a new resort in our area will open soon.

_____    5. For many years the people of Salt Lake City have been
_____        downhill skiing at another popular place Park City Ski Area.

_____    6. John my cousin from L.A. went to college in Massachusetts.

_____    7. My brother's employer Mr. Franklin called at our house last
_____        night.

_____    8. Juneau is the capital of Alaska the largest state in the union.

_____    9. On the Fourth of July my favorite holiday we always watch
_____        the fireworks display.

_____    10. Our final number "Purple People Eater" is dedicated to all
_____        extraterrestrials in attendance.

_____    11. The sign one I'd put up had blown down.

_____    12. No one least of all Marsha realized the importance of the
_____        event.

_____    13. Her favorite cologne "Eau d'Elephant" was on sale.

_____    14. Leon's trip to England included a visit to one or early man's
_____        great achievements Stonehenge.

# Review

Directions: Use periods, question marks, and exclamation points and the necessary commas in the following sentences.

1. Because the meeting is scheduled for Tuesday I'll arrive in town on Monday June 16 at four o'clock
2. Herman Melville author of *Moby Dick* was born in New York New York in 1819
3. If it is ten o'clock in Maine what time is it in Chicago
4. Oh don't forget to include your name address and phone number on the card
5. According to this information sheet you used to live at 120 Clover Street Cleveland Ohio.

Directions: Rewrite the following sentences, adding the necessary punctuation.

1. Did you know that William son of Prince Charles and Princess Diana was given four names.

_____

_____

2. While reading about Rome Tony a recent American immigrant realized how much he missed his homeland Italy.

_____

_____

3. By Wednesday October 7 1993 I predict that Venice California will have sunk into the Pacific Ocean.

_____

_____

# Commas with Quotation Marks

A comma is used *before* quotation marks.

    Example: Dorothy said, "I'd like to go home," in a voice so soft it could barely be heard.

If the sentence ends with the quotation, then any other necessary punctuation comes *before* the ending quotation marks.

    Example: Connie asked, "Where are you going?"
             Bud yelled, "Watch out!"
             Monica remarked, "I've seen that movie."

Directions: Read each sentence and place commas and end punctuation in the proper spots. The write any words that precede commas on the blanks to the left.

    Example:   __stated__      Greg stated, "I thought you'd left," when he saw Bob nearby.

              __left__

           __replied__      Bob replied, "I'm still here."

_____    1. The sign proclaimed "No Smoking" in bold letters.

_____

_____

_____

_____

_____

_____

_____

_____

_____

_____

_____

_____

_____

_____

_____

2. Miss Johnson queried the class "Do all of you understand this principle"

3. Mark surprised them by saying "I'm resigning as president" shortly before school was to open.

4. Lee crowed "I'm going to get an A on this test" as he filled in another wrong answer.

5. Linda whispered urgently "I can't seem to find my homework"

6. "No one has seen Freddy for days" reported Xavier.

7. The coach suggested "Try that new play we worked on yesterday" when the team had fallen behind.

8. Claudette rasped "I think I've got strep throat" while she boiled water for tea.

9. "Be sure" announced Mr. Richardson to his class "that you bring a pen to class"

10. The beautician lamented "I'll have to refund your money" as she looked down at her customer's bald head.

Directions: Copy the following sentences, carefully adding commas and end punctuation.

1. "Everyone" said Glenda "seems to have done very well"

_____

_____

2. Dad asked "Don't you think I was your age once"

_____

_____

3. Bruce mumbled "I thought we had a date" in a tone that reflected his disappointment.

_____

_____

Directions: Clearly mark the necessary end punctuation and commas in the following sentences.

1. Wow I already know ten rules of punctuation seven of them dealing with commas
2. Mr. Jenkins my English teacher said "I'll bet you will know all of them before June 1990"
3. "Well" I thought "at least I'll know *most* of them by then"
4. My friend asked later "Does anyone really know all that stuff"
5. "They do" I answered "if they want to get a passing grade on the final"

Directions: For extra credit, copy the following sentences and add commas and end punctuation. Include periods after abbreviations.

1. "My plan" said Phil Holochek "is to create a ski area for families"

_____

_____

2. He opened Shasta Ski Park on Mt. Shasta in the fall of 1985

_____

_____

3. Because his area is so successful he created a ski club for families in January 1987 for the Mt. Shasta and Redding California areas

_____

_____

# Commas in Compound Sentences

In the following sentences, underline the verbs twice and their subjects once.

> Doris ran to the swimming pool.
> She jumped in.

Did you underline this way? <u>Doris ran</u> to the swimming pool. <u>She jumped</u> in. Good!

So far you've been working with simple sentences. Now, you're ready for compound sentences. A compound sentence is two complete sentences joined by one of these words: *and, but, or, nor, yet,* or *for* (when *for* mean *because.*) Put a comma between the two complete sentences.

> Examples: *Doris ran* to the swimming pool, and *she jumped* in.
> *She remembered* to wear a cap, but *she forgot* to change into her suit.
> *Should she put* on her suit, or *should she continue* to swim in her dress?

In each example, there is a separate subject and verb both before and after the conjunction. (*And, but,* and *or* a conjunctions.) If the second part of the sentence does not have a subject, the sentence is not compound, and it doesn't need a comma.

Look back at the third example. *She* is a subject twice. How many times is *she* the subject in the following sentence? _____ (number)

> Example: *Should she put* on her suit or *continue* to swim in her dress?

*She* is only the subject once in that example. Since the sentence has only one subject, it cannot possibly be compound. You see, *compound* means "two or more."

Directions: See if you can correctly fill in the following blanks by using the information above.

Compound sentences are usually _____ (how many?) sentences joined by

using the _____, _____, _____

_____, _____, _____, or

_____. The three words most commonly used to create compound sentences

are _____, _____, and _____

_____.

If a sentence is compound, it must have at least _____ separate subjects that

have their own verbs. The two separate sentences are joined by a _____

(what kind of word?) *Compound* means "_____".

It's essential that you be able to tell the difference between sentences that are compound and those that aren't. To decide, the best idea is to find and underline the *verbs* and their *subjects*. A sentence is compound if it's got a separate subject and verb both before and after one of the six conjunctions. If it doesn't, the sentence is called "simple."

Directions: In each sentence below, underline the verb(s) twice and the subject(s) once. If the sentence has two separate subjects and their verbs, write *compound* on the blank line. If it doesn't, write *simple* on the line. In compound sentences only, put a comma *before* the conjunction.

Examples: _____simple_____ a. *Mary* and *Joan* were *walking* through the steamy rain forest. (only one main verb: *walking*)

_____compound_____ b. *Mary* and *Joan walked* through the forest, but *they could* not *find* the trees.

_____ 1. We were five miles from home and low on gas but not a gas station was open.

_____ 2. We can to the corner of Fourth and Main and the motor went dead.

_____ 3. Rosemary opened the door and called for her pet alligator to come home.

_____ 4. The whole family tried to assist him but he refused their help.

_____ 5. Is he just stupid or does he have a reason for his behavior?

_____ 6. I walked the lonely street alone yet I felt another presence somewhere nearby.

_____ 7. No one knew nor cared about his situation.

_____ 8. They either dropped anchor off the Florida coast or went on to Jamaica.

_____ 9. I liked the new adventure film and I told all my friends about it.

_____ 10. The show ended at 10 p.m. but I didn't get home until midnight.

_____ 11. The top of the mountain gave us a panoramic view of the valley and the hills below but we could see no lights of Asheville.

_____ 12. The trees had become one yet they each swayed separately in the wind.

_____ 13. Our group had been climbing the mountain since morning and no bears had been seen or heard the whole way.

_____ 14. We were alert but we were not frightened.

_____ 15. The bears had to come out of hibernation soon or they would die of thirst and starvation.

Directions: First, underline the <u>verb</u> and the <u>subject</u>. Second, place a comma in the sentence if necessary. Third, on the blank line write either the word that precedes the comma or write *no comma*.

Examples: ___car___  a. We <u>have</u> a car, but <u>we</u> <u>decided</u> to walk to the store.

___no comma___  b. <u>Glen</u> <u>took</u> a deep breath and <u>tried</u> again.

_____ 1. I read *Childhood's End* and *Rendezvous with Rama* by Arthur C. Clarke.

_____ 2. Clarke is not only a novelist but he is also a scientist.

_____ 3. Maxine prefers stories of adventure and romance to those about space travel.

_____ 4. Science fiction often includes adventure and romance yet Maxine will not read Clarke.

_____ 5. Either Maxine has a closed mind or she is not yet mature enough to enjoy some books.

_____ 6. Troy stopped by the library for he knew he owed money for an overdue book.

_____ 7. The librarian asked him for his name and the book's due date.

_____ 8. Troy knew his name but he had forgotten the due date.

_____ 9. The librarian checked the records and told him the amount of the fine.

_____ 10. Troy had enough money to pay the fine and he even had extra money for lunch.

# Noun in Direct Address

When you speak directly to someone and use that person's name, you must separate the name from the rest of the sentence with commas. This is called noun in direct address.

Example: *John*, are you ready to leave?
I think, *Sarah*, it's time to go.

The same rule is true even when you address a thing such as a pet or other object.

Example: Come over here and lie down, *dog*!
Please, *car*, start.

Notice that the person or object that you are addressing comes within the sentence, you set it off with commas by putting commas on each side of it.

Directions: In the blank to the left write the noun that is being addressed and should, therefore, be set off with a comma or commas.

Example:      Bob     1. Bob how long will you be staying in New York?

    bird     2. Get out of that cat food bird!

    team     3. Okay team let's go out there and win one for old Newark High.

_____  1. Listen gang we can pull this caper off if everyone does his job.

_____  2. Have you seen Mary today Michael?

_____  3. I can't for the life of me figure out Donnie why you're not taking Spanish this year.

_____  4. Mr. Slone do we have to do this assignment tonight?

_____  5. Charlie did you know that the World Trade Center is the tallest building in the United States?

_____  6. If I can have your attention students I'll show you how to use this computer.

_____  7. Now boys and girls take out your pencils and we'll do our maps of London.

_____  8. Please television don't go out right during the best part of the movie.

_____  9. Algebra you'd drive a same person crazy!

_____  10. That shirt might come back into style Dad if you keep it long enough.

_____  11. I love you dearly Sweetheart.

_____  12. Come on legs and hold up for just a few more miles and we'll win this race.

_____  13. Honest Mr. Hollahan. My mother did wash my homework assignment.

_____  14. If you cross one more time skis I'll use you for firewood.

Directions: On the blank line provided, write the letter of the sentence that is correctly punctuated.

_____  1. a. We jumped and shouted and waved our banners as the team took the field.
        b. We jumped, and shouted, and waved our banners as the team took the field.

_____ 2. a. Write to Mrs. J.R. Ewing, 211 South Fork Avenue, Dallas, Texas 10010, for information.
b. Write to, Mrs. J.R. Ewing, 211 South Fork Avenue, Dallas Texas 10010, for information.

_____ 3. a. Joe entered the room first and Donna came in later.
b. Joe entered the room first, and Donna came in later.

_____ 4. a. The students sell popcorn, soft drinks, and cookies at Nova's dances.
b. The students sell popcorn, soft drinks, and cookies, at Nova's dances.

_____ 5. a. When they finally ended the game it was dark.
b. When they finally ended the game, it was dark.

_____ 6. a. I found a book dated, December 2, 1969, in our library.
b. I found a book dated December 2, 1969, in our library.

_____ 7. a. I chased the dog into the yard, and it barked at the cat.
b. I chased the dog into the yard and it barked at the cat.

_____ 8. a. After they are weaned, dogs can be given to a good home.
b. After they are weaned dogs can be given to a good home.

_____ 9. a. We ate watermelon, hot dogs, and potato salad, at the picnic.
b. We ate watermelon, hot dogs, and potato salad at the picnic.

_____ 10. a. We cooked, and cleaned, and washed clothes almost every Monday at camp.
b. We cooked and cleaned and washed clothes almost every Monday at camp.

_____ 11. a. Saturn High School, 2200 Feldspar Way, Kingsport, Maine 96001, is a great school.
b. Saturn High School, 2200 Feldspar Way, Kingsport, Maine 96001, is a great school.

_____ 12. a. Reagan was elected on November 6, 1980 for his first term.
b. Reagan was elected on November 6, 1980, for his first term.

_____ 13. a. Well, did he say, "I need it", or didn't he?
b. Well, did he say, "I need it," or didn't he?

_____ 14. a. Because of good grades, she won a scholarship to Harvard.
b. Because of good grades she won a scholarship to Harvard.

_____ 15. a. Jerry Dangl, director of student programs said, "Students need to take more math."
b. Jerry Dangl, director of student programs, said, "Students need to take more math."

Directions: Add necessary end punctuation and commas to the remaining sentences.

1. "Yes I saw the stop sign but my brakes failed" said Tom earnestly
2. Is that address still 567 Bleacher Road Islington Texas 60640
3. My parents' anniversary party will be held on Sunday August 14 1983
4. Brian a would-be actor took singing lessons and attended drama classes
5. Well are you going to spend the weekend at home or will you go to Aunt Jenny's place

90

# Quotation Marks

Use quotation marks only around someone's *exact words*.

> Examples: "I just knew that you'd come back," said Count Dracula.
> "I just knew," said Count Dracula, "that you'd come back."

A common mistake that students make is to use quotation marks even when someone's exact words aren't used.

> Example: Count Dracula said "he knew you'd come back." (WRONG) Oops! Dracula never said the word *he*, so quotation marks shouldn't be used at all.

> Example: Count Dracula said he knew that you'd come back. (RIGHT!)

Directions: Add the missing quotation marks and commas to the following sentences. (Don't forget that commas, periods, etc. go before quotation marks.) Not all sentences require quotation marks.

1. Barbara yelled Get out of the boat!
2. Let's jump groaned Joanie before it's too late.
3. The green parrot asked what Polly wanted.
4. The blue parrot answered Polly wants a cracker.
5. Why can't I play Colleen inquired.
6. Because Kristine answered I'm afraid you'll get hurt.
7. Wow Colleen retorted that's the craziest thing I've heard.
8. Kristine looked startled and said I just thought I'd look out for you.
9. Colleen said not to worry about her.
10. I'll play if I want to she thought.
11. Let's have our Frisbee contest at the park said Heather.
12. Isn't the park too crowded? asked Brad
13. Heather said that the park was not crowded at the north end.
14. She added Besides we're having the contest on Wednesday.
15. Brad told her to proceed with her plans.
16. Besides he said maybe other people would like to watch.
17. She asked what he had for prizes.
18. A picture of my dad, his autograph, and a pass to Kangaroo Courts responded Brad.
19. Didn't you get his latest book? inquired Heather
20. Brad replied that not many people want to read about bicycling for health.

Use quotation marks around titles of things that are quite short: short stories, articles, or chapters. Use underlining to indicate titles of things that are long: books, plays, magazines, newspapers. Never use both quotation marks and underlining for the same title. In printed material, long titles aren't underlined — they appear in italics.

> Example: "The Unicorn in the Garden" is a humorous story from *Fables for Our Times* by James Thurber.

Directions: Decide whether the title in each sentence is of something short, necessitating quotation marks, or something long, requiring underlining. Use the correct marking in the sentence and then put *QM* (for quotation marks) or *U* (for underlining) on the blank lines.

> Example: _____U_____    The article appeared in *Time*.

_____    1. Shakespeare's tragic play Romeo and Juliet is one of his most popular works.

_____    2. I subscribe to the Record Searchlight, a local paper.

_____ 3. Outlooks is the title of the book used in class by many teachers.

_____ 4. One story I especially like is The Most Dangerous Game.

_____ 5. The article, called YRU FATT, was written by Richard Simmons, a TV personality.

_____ 6. Who's Who is a book you can use to find out about famous living people.

_____ 7. Doris Lessing wrote the short story A Sunrise on the Veld about her experiences in Africa.

_____ 8. Annie was a popular Broadway show that later became a movie.

_____ 9. In my diet book the chapter entitled Do it Yourself Jaw-wiring has been most helpful.

_____ 10. The setting of Peter Beagle's novel A Fine and Private Place is, believe it or not, a cemetery.

_____ 11. I bought a book called Photography Made Easy.

_____ 12. Night Pictures is the chapter I liked best.

_____ 13. Do you know the author of the book The Princess Bride?

_____ 14. My cousin subscribes to National Geographic.

_____ 15. The Lottery, by Shirley Jackson, is a short story with a surprise conclusion.

# Review

Directions: Rewrite and punctuate the following sentences correctly, using quotation marks, underlining, end punctuation, and commas.

1. Professor Adams my instructor asked Do you expect to pass your examination

_____

_____

2. Bring the package into the kitchen Mother shouted

_____

_____

3. How is your sister Jane inquired

_____

_____

4. I asked the cabin attendant why we are not able to land now

_____

_____

5. I shall be fifteen on September 15 1983 declared Julio

_____

_____

6. My parents ordered Natural History a nature magazine with a lot of beautiful pictures

_____

_____

7. The class heard Edgar Allan Poe's The Telltale Heart a spooky story about murder and madness

_____

_____

# Apostrophes

Use an apostrophe to show where letters have been left out of shortened words. I'll (*sha* or *wi* is left out); we're (*a* is left out); o'clock (*of the clock* is shortened); shouldn't (*o* is left out). The word *won't* is short for *will not*.

Directions: In the following exercises, put apostrophes in the shortened words. Then write the words with apostrophes on the blank lines. (Not all blanks will be filled.)

Example: ____I'll____     I'll meet you at

____o'clock____     eight o'clock tomorrow.

_____     1. I dont think youve done that problem correctly.

_____     2. Youre crazy about pizza, arent you?

_____     3. I cant believe shed do that.

_____     4. Well be leaving at twelve oclock.

_____     5. Ive improved my math grade recently

_____     6. Youll accompany me to the party, wont you?

_____     7. Ted couldnt remember his own phone number.

_____     8. If youd like to go, Ill make the arrangements.

_____     9. Im not sure that hed approve of that idea.

_____   10. Weve been having a great time, havent we?

_____   11. Theyre expecting me at three, but Ill be late.

_____   12. Someones in that shadowy corner!

_____   13. Id been told he wasnt home yet.

_____   14. Lynns finished the test, but Im not done.

_____   15. Thats the silliest costume youve ever worn.

_____

   Use an apostrophe to show ownership or possession. Sounds simple enough, doesn't it? It is simple if you can remember one basis rule: add an apostrophe and an *s* after the word that "possesses" something.

Example: The *dog's* nose was cool and wet.
   The *dogs'* noses were cool and wet.
   The *children's* noses were cool and wet.

In the first example, the owner of the nose, the dog, is followed by *'s*. In the second example, the word is *dogs*, and dogs is followed by *'s*. Notice that since the word ends in *s*, the *s* after the apostrophe is optional. In the third example, the word is *children*, and it is followed by *'s*.

In the following examples, underline the possessive words (the owner or owners).

   1. Johns car.
   2. a cats dish
   3. the ants nests
   4. the womens tournaments.

Did you underline *John*, *cats*, *ants*, and *women*? Then you know that the correct phrases are John's car, a cat's disk, the ants' (ants's) nests, and the women's tournaments.

Directions: Each of the following phrases needs an apostrophe. First, decide what the possessive word is and underline it. Then, on the line, write the word, adding *'s*.

Example:  ___girls'___   some <u>girls</u> shoes.

_____   1. the clowns face

_____   2. the young mans car

_____   3. the foxs nose

_____   4. many boats sails

_____   5. the horses manes

_____   6. the subways tracks

_____   7. a matchs flame

_____  8. several rabbits tails

_____  9. that shirts buttons

_____  10. the mans whiskers

Directions: Follow the same directions from the last exercise. Also add the apostrophe in the phrase.

    Example: ___skier's___  the skier's broken leg.

_____  1. all teachers gradebooks

_____  2. the families houses

_____  3. a dimes worth

_____  4. two hours time

_____  5. a boys book

_____  6. several students assignments

_____  7. the Smiths cabin

_____  8. nobodys fault

_____  9. the girls gym (for all girls)

_____  10. a moments hesitation

Directions: Change the following phrases to possessive phrases using apostrophes.

    Example: ___the babies'(s) bottles___  the bottles of the babies

_____  1. the teeth of the wolves

_____  2. the tires on the truck

_____  3. the pages of the book

_____  4. the gloves of the ladies

_____  5. the legs of the chair

_____  6. a club for women

_____  7. a painting by Rembrandt

_____  8. the bulletin for today

_____  9. the discoveries of Madame Curie

_____  10. the victories of the athletes

    For extra credit, write a five-sentence paragraph about a favorite toy from your childhood. The paragraph should contain at least three correct possessive phrases containing apostrophes.

Directions: Read each sentence and decide which word or words require apostrophes. Put the apostrophe in the sentence and then rewrite the words with apostrophes on the blanks.

_____

_____    1. Theyre going to Mikes house.

_____    2. Whats happening in Mrs. Jones chemistry class?

_____    3. The football players ran a lap and then went into the boys locker room.

_____    4. Weve had so many pets that we could have filled Noahs ark.

_____    5. In spring, its said, a young mans fancy turns to thoughts of love.

_____    6. I cant believe Rachels excuse for not having her homework.

_____    7. Marty shouldnt stay out past eleven oclock.

_____    8. While in Virginia, the Johnsons will visit Mt. Vernon, Washingtons home.

_____    9. My parents favorite TV show was "Lets Make a Deal."

_____    10. I saw a T-shirt that proclaimed, "A womans place is in the house — and the senate!"

Directions: Write the letter of the sentence that does not have an error in the use of apostrophes.

_____    1. a. Earls' report was about a farmer's daily life.
              b. Earl's report was about a farmer's daily life.
              c. Earl's report was about a farmers' daily life.

_____ 2. a. The team's victory was due to two boy's playing.
       b. The teams' victory was due to two boys' playing.
       c. The team's victory was due to two boys' playing.

_____ 3. a. Tomorrow's paper will contain all the winners' names.
       b. Tomorrows paper will contain all the winners' names.
       c. Tomorrows' paper will contain all the winner's names.

_____ 4. a. The children's sleep was disturbed by a dogs' barking.
       b. The childrens' sleep was disturbed by a dog's barking.
       c. The children's sleep was disturbed by a dog's barking.

_____ 5. a. A pilot's first duty is to consider all passengers' safety.
       b. A pilots' first duty is to consider all passengers' safety.
       c. A pilot's first duty is to consider all passenger's safety.

_____ 6. a. Two boy's mothers made all the children's lunches.
       b. Two boys' mothers made all the children's lunches.
       c. Two boys' mothers made all the childrens' lunches.

_____ 7. a. Several pupil's papers were on the teacher's desk.
       b. Several pupils' papers were on the teachers' desk.
       c. Several pupils' papers were on the teacher's desk.

_____ 8. a. This girl's job is to check all the men's wraps.
       b. This girl's job is to check all the mens' wraps.
       c. This girls' job is to check all the men's wraps.

_____ 9. a. He isn't sure that it's safe.
       b. He isent sure that its' safe.
       c. He is'nt sure that its safe.

_____ 10. a. We're afraid he does'nt know.
        b. We're afraid he dosent know.
        c. We're afraid he doesn't know.

_____ 11. a. Let's see if they're at home.
        b. Lets see if they're at home.
        c. Lets' see if there're at home.

_____ 12. a. Who's the boy who cann't swim?
        b. Who'se the boy who can't swim?
        c. Who's the boy who can't swim?

Directions: Each sentence contains one word from which the apostrophe should be omitted. Write this word, omitting the apostrophe.

_____ 1. The Brown's don't like dogs.

_____ 2. Let's not open the gift's before Christmas.

_____ 3. Helen's sweater is just like your's and Linda's.

_____ 4. Our neighbor's tree extend's over our roof.

_____ 5. Jerry put it's food in one of Mother's best dishes.

_____ 6. The Harts' new car won't be delivered for three days.

Directions: Write the correct word in each of the two pairs.

_____

_____

1. (It's, Its) usually in (its, it's) nest at this time.

_____

2. (They're, Their) lights are always on when (they're, their) at home.

_____

3. (Your, You're) always changing (your, you're) mind.

_____

4. (Whose, Who's) the girl (whose, who's) poster won?

_____

5. (Let's, Lets) see if he (let's, lets) us help him.

_____

6. (It's Its) better not to drive when (you're, your) tired.

_____

7. (They're, Their) pleased with (your, you're) gift.

# Capitalization

The first rules of capitalization will be familiar to you.

Rule 1: Capitalize the first word of every sentence, the pronoun *I*, and the first word of a direct quotation.

Example: The commander shouted, "You will do what I say!"

Directions: Underline each word that should be capitalized and then write those words on the lines to the left. Be sure to capitalize the words when you write them. (There won't be a word for every blank.)

Example:    **A**     a man told me, "<u>don't</u> think <u>i</u> won't succeed."

       Don't

       I

1. my teacher asked, "what did i just tell you?"

2. someone said, "it's a spaceship! where did it come from?"

3. "i'm in high school this year," stated the boy.

4. "one thing i enjoy," she said, "is playing computer games."

5. "you're right!" the instructor exclaimed. "that's the first correct answer i've had all day."

Rule 2: Capitalize a person's name, a title used as part of a person's name, and names referring to sacred writings or the Deity.

Example: Mr. Yamamoto asked Peter if he was familiar with the old Testament.

Directions: Underline each word that should be capitalized and then write those words on the lines to the left.

_____

_____

_____

_____

_____

_____

_____

_____

_____

_____

_____

_____

_____

_____

_____

_____

_____

1. I learned that president lincoln was married to mary todd.

2. From his bible, pastor thomas read, "So god created man in his own image."

3. My mother asked miss garcia if she had met dr. schmidt.

4. Mrs. wong, who is the principal of our school, asked professor dolan to speak at the assembly.

5. The rolling stones is one rock group event aunt susan remembers.

Rule 3: Capitalize days of the week, months of the year, and holidays.

Example: Because of the Memorial Day holiday, there was no school on the first Monday of June.

Directions: Underline each word that should be capitalized and then write those words on the lines to the left.

_____

_____

_____

_____

_____

1. During july and august, I visit the library every tuesday.

2. In the fall we celebrate labor day and thanksgiving.

_____

_____

_____

_____

_____

_____

_____

3. Next year, is easter during march or april?

4. On the fourth of july, I walked to the park to see the fireworks.

5. Our class will go to the planetarium on wednesday or thursday.

Rule 4: Capitalize the names of geographical places, important buildings, and historical objects and events.

Examples: The Liberty Bell may be seen near Independence Hall in Philadelphia, Pennsylvania.

Directions: Underline each word that should be capitalized and then write those words on the lines to the left.

_____

_____

_____

_____

_____

_____

_____

_____

_____

_____

_____

_____

_____

_____

1. Even folks from oregon go to lake shasta for summer vacations.

2. In the west they have the sacramento river as well as yosemite.

3. Everyone knows that the white house is in washington, d.c.

4. The battle of britain took place during world war II.

5. A rough draft of the declaration of independence may be found in the library of congress.

Rule 5: Capitalize the first word and chief words in titles of books and the brand names of products, but *not* the products.

Examples: Following the article entitled "Waves of Change," there is an ad for Swift binoculars.

Directions: Underline each word that should be capitalized and then write those words on the lines to the left.

_____

_____

_____

_____

_____

_____

_____

_____

_____

_____

1. One of Steinbeck's shorter novels is *of mice and men.*

2. He decided on a manhattan shirt and some big brother jeans.

3. The title of the poetry book is *reflections on a gift of watermelon pickle.*

4. As a joke, we filled my uncle's ford station wagon with dry quaker oatmeal.

5. The short story "the lady or the tiger?" is quite intriguing.

Rule 6: Capitalize proper adjectives. Capitalize school subjects only if followed by numbers or it they are languages.

Example: Next year I'll take Algebra I, American history, and Spanish.

Directions: Underline each word that should be capitalized and then write those words on the lines to the left.

_____

_____

_____

_____

_____

_____

_____

_____

1. Betty is getting high grades in english, mathematics, and home economics II.

2. Would you prefer french or russian dressing on your salad?

3. The chinese delegate to the conference had italian spaghetti for lunch.

4. In college I'll major in biology, but I also plan to take european history, geology, and psychology.

5. Pat expects to pass band I, geography, german III, and literature.

Directions: Suppose that each of the following phrases occurred within a sentence. Write the letter of the one phrase in each group that is correctly capitalized.

_____ 1. a. the old greek ruins
b. the old Greek Ruins
c. the old Greek ruins

_____ 2. a. use Ajax Cleanser
b. use ajax cleanser
c. use Ajax cleanser

_____ 3. a. the United Finance company
b. the United Finance Company
c. the United finance company

_____ 4. a. the World Trade center
b. the World Trade Center
c. the World trade center

_____ 5. a. in a Redding Restaurant
b. in a Redding restaurant
c. in a redding restaurant

_____ 6. a. the song was "Kissin' In The Kitchen"
b. the song was "Kissin' in the Kitchen"
c. the song was "Kissin' In the Kitchen"

_____ 7. a. in the Cascade theater
b. in the Cascade Theater
c. in the cascade theater

_____ 8. a. with the English class
b. with the English Class
c. with the english class

_____ 9. a. I saw my Grandfather
b. I saw my grandfather
c. i saw my grandfather

_____ 10. a. in High School
b in High school
c. in high school

_____ 11. a. at Bailey high school
b. at Bailey High school
c. at Bailey High School

_____ 12. a. boating on Big Stone lake
b. boating on Big Stone Lake
c. boating on big stone lake

_____ 13. a. eating christmas breakfast
b. eating Christmas Breakfast
c. eating Christmas breakfast

_____ 14. a. the Senate Hiking club
b. the Senate hiking club
c. the Senate Hiking Club

_____ 15. a. the Springfield baptist church
b. the Springfield Baptist church
c. the Springfield Baptist Church

_____ 16. a. any Baptist church
b. any baptist church
c. any Baptist Church

_____ 17. a. the new Spring clothes
              b. the new spring clothes
              c. the new spring Clothes

_____ 18. a. the book, *The Grapes Of Wrath*
              b. the book, *the Grapes of Wrath*
              c. the book, *The Grapes of Wrath*

_____ 19. a. a Honda motorcycle
              b. a Honda Motorcycle
              c. a honda Motorcycle

_____ 20. a. on Memorial day
              b. on Memorial Day
              c. on memorial day

**Directions:** In the blanks, write the letters of all words that should be capitalized.

                    A   B      C

_____ 1. This fall uncle Sam's lake was full.

              A      B           C   D    E   F

_____ 2. My dad is a teacher for the McGregor union high school district.

                 A              B                        C

_____ 3. Our principal invited professor Cerreta to speak about our local college.

             A                           B          C

_____ 4. coach McCasland was praised by the sports editor of the Times searchlight.

                 A          B             C         D

_____ 5. Many people in our community think my mother looks like aunt Evelyn.

             A  B                 C        D

_____ 6. My high school will celebrate Memorial day next wednesday.

                    A   B             C         D

_____ 7. The Evergreen hiking club will hike in Central park on our next holiday.

                        A     B        C       D           E

_____ 8. I have a picture of my aunts, uncles, and cousins from uncle Joe's reunion last june
                      F
             in nebraska.

                    A          B           C   D   E

_____ 9. My mother gave grandfather Gibbons a kodak movie camera for his birthday.

                 A       B   C   D     E    F

_____ 10. My dad likes french fried potatoes and spanish omelettes for breakfast.

**Directions:** In the blank, write the letter of the sentence that is correctly punctuated and capitalized.

_____ 1. a. The boy said, "That the skiing is great today."
             b. The boy said that the skiing is great today.

_____ 2. a. The coach emphasized, "Football is the game of life."
             b. The coach emphasized football is the game of life.

_____ 3. a. "This is a time of tribulation", began the valedictorian.
             b. "This is a time of tribulation," began the valedictorian.

_____ 4. a. "What else can you add?," asked the teacher.
             b. "What else can you add?" asked the teacher.

_____ 5. a. Mr. Muir announced, "Your test was a disaster."
             b. Mr. Muir announced, "your test was a disaster."

_____ 6. a. "Did you pass?" asked Mike.
b. "Did you pass," asked Mike?

_____ 7. a. "What a beautiful girl," shouted Reginald?
b. "What a beautiful girl!" shouted Reginald.

_____ 8. a. The little girl asked, "Why do horses whinny through their noses?"
b. The little girl asked, "Why do horses whinny through their noses"?

Directions: Add punctuation and capital letters to the following pieces of writing. Rewrite each sentence correctly.

1. id like to see the coach screamed the angry parent

_____

_____

2. im the coach said mr. howard

_____

_____

3. why arent you playing my son shouted the parent hes one of youre best players

_____

_____

4. because said coach howard your son quit the team a week ago

_____

_____

5. are you going to the nova high school dance this weekend asked mark

_____

_____

6. no replied mike im tired of high school dances

_____

_____

7. you cant mean that argued mark youre not short of money are you

_____

_____

8. no mike replied im just shy about asking girls to dance

_____

_____

# Spelling

This section of your text-workbook focuses on spelling. The words that you'll study fit two categories. Those in the first category are words that students often misspell. The second category of words includes those that are used often, especially by high school students.

Because all the words in this section are either often misspelled, often used, or both, it's worthwhile for you to learn them. The first step is to memorize the spelling of the word. But the most important step is to use the word correctly. Then the spelling and meaning of the word will stay with you.

Directions: Read this list of words, word pairs, and word groups. These are words that are commonly misspelled or misused. Read the explanations carefully. They have hints that will make spelling them correctly easier.

| | | |
|---|---|---|
| *1.* | **a lot** | Two words. (I like English *a* whole *lot*.) If this were one word, what would you do with "whole"? |
| *2.* | **there** | Opposite of *here*. (Put the package down over *there*.) Remember: t+*here* = there |
| | **their** | Ownership. (Purple, gold, and white are *their* colors.) heir — one who *owns* something when she or he inherits it; t+*heir* = their |
| | **they're** | They are. (*They're* winning the game.) Remember: An apostrophe takes the place of a missing letter. Here the *a* is missing in "are." |
| *3.* | **to** | Toward. (He went *to* the store.) |
| | **too** | Also or excessively — *too* much, *too* hot, *too* big. (This test is *too* difficult for me.) |
| | **two** | One more than one; the number two. (She had *two* books for the same class.) |
| *4.* | **etc.** | Et cetera, a Latin abbreviation meaning "and so on." (A good student always has a pen, paper, books, *etc.*) |
| *5.* | **threw** | Past tense of *to throw*. (He *threw* a fit in geography.) |
| | **through** | A preposition meaning to pass into and out of something. (She put the thread *through* the eye of the needle.) Also, to be done with. (He is *through* with his work.) |
| *6.* | **your** | Ownership. (That is *your* paper on the floor.) |
| | **you're** | You are. *You're* never too old to enjoy snow skiing. Remember: The apostrophe takes the place of a missing letter. Here the *a* is missing. |
| *7.* | **no** | Opposite of yes. (*No*, I won't do it! He has no *paper*.) |
| | **know** | To be familiar with something. (I *know* her from school.) |
| | **now** | Immediately. (He wants the money *now*.) |

Directions: Look at the sentences below. If any one of the words from the previous list is spelled incorrectly, spell it correctly in the blank. If all words are spelled correctly, write *okay* in the blank.

_____ 1. A lot of students in high school think that there classes are boring.

_____ 2. They say that when your sitting in class the teachers talk too much.

_____ 3. We all know that might be true, since they talk about homework, rules, books, etc.

_____ 4. There is no way a student can absorb everything they're saying.

_____ 5. Teachers need to get that threw there heads.

_____

6. Really, a student should only have two classes a day, as we all now.

_____

7. Then, they could get threw their school day earlier.

_____

8. That way they would have a lot of time to watch MTV, etc.

_____

9. Students really should have more free time of they're own.

_____

10. You're free time is to valuable too be taken with a lot of school work, chores, etc.

# Spelling Quiz #1

Directions: Circle the correct word.

1. He had books, pen, paper, notebooks (etc. ect.) on his first day of school.

2. The top shelf was (to, too, two) high for her to reach.

3. The principal wants to see you (now, know).

4. When he asked her to dance, she said, "(No, Know)."

5. (Alot, A lot) of her money is spent on her hobby, sailboarding.

6. While she was (there, their, they're), Joan took many pictures of Hawaii.

7. The message said that (your, you're) to report to the office immediately.

8. Because she had (to, too, two) invitations to the prom, she was very excited.

9. Yesterday, his horse (threw, through) a shoe.

10. Students in English usually have (there, their they're) essays written by Friday.

11. Bernard went (to, too, two) the store for his grandmother.

12. Please, have (your, you're) tickets ready when you get to the door.

13. If you pass (threw, through) that gate, you'll be close to your seats.

14. Did she (no, now, know) the answer to problem five?

15. Although (there, their, they're) the oldest living thing on earth, the bristlecone pine tree has been seen by relatively few people.

This list of words causes many people trouble because it's made up of homonyms, Homonyms are words that sound alike but aren't spelled alike. Look at these homonyms. Check the meaning of each one and the example sentence. They will help you to know when to use each one.

| | |
|---|---|
| **already** | Happened in the past or before. (We have _already_ had this word.) |
| **all ready** | Prepared; everything is ready. (They are _all ready_ for the test.) |
| **vary** | Change. (He is going to _vary_ his throwing style.) |
| **very** | To a great degree. (That test is _very_ hard.) |
| **right** | Correct; opposite of left. (That answer is the _right_ answer.) |
| **write** | To form letters and words. (I'm going to _write_ a letter to my brother.) |
| **by** | Next to. (The tennis court is _by_ the gym.) |
| **bye** | A shortened form of _good-bye_. (She said, "Bye," as the group left.) |
| **buy** | To pay for something. (He went to the store to _buy_ milk.) |

| | |
|---|---|
| **its** | Ownership form of it; note the lack of an apostrophe. (The plane dumped *its* fuel before landing.) |
| **it's** | It plus is; the apostrophe takes the place of the missing "i." (*It's* all the work that I object to.) |
| **knew** | Past tense of *know*. (He *knew* that girl from somewhere.) |
| **new** | Not old. (We bought a *new* car.) |
| **here** | In this place; opposite of *there*. (Place your homework *here*.) |
| **hear** | Listen with the ears; note the word *ear* in the word *hear*. (He asked for quiet so that he could *hear* the speaker.) |
| **lets** | Allows; give permission to. (He *lets* us use his swimming pool.) |
| **let's** | Let plus us; the apostrophe takes the place of the missing "u." (*Let's* go for a walk in the park.) |
| **were** | Have been. (We *were* in the eighth grade last year.) |
| **we're** | We plus are. (*We're* going to pass this class.) |
| **wear** | To put clothes or other items on a body. (She wants to *wear* the red blouse today.) |
| **where** | In or at what place? (*Where* did you park your motorcycle?) |
| **brakes** | Objects that stop something in motion. (She applied the *brakes* of her moped to come to a stop.) |
| **breaks** | Lucky happenings; destroys something. (She gets all the *breaks* in English. She *breaks* a record every time she runs the mile.) |
| **road** | Usually a place where a car is driven. (The *road* to the ski resort is steep.) |
| **rode** | Past tense of *ride*. (Yesterday, he *rode* his bike to school.) |
| **coarse** | Rough. (Sandpaper is *coarse*.) |
| **course** | A subject; an area for play; a plan. (Spanish is a tough *course*. The golf *course* is a nice place to spend an afternoon. He set his *course* for the future.) |
| **weather** | Rain, sun, or snow. (The *weather* in Phoenix in the summer is usually hot.) |
| **whether** | An word indicating alternatives. (I don't know *whether* to study or to watch MTV.) |
| **hole** | An empty spot. (He dug a *hole* in the ground.) |
| **whole** | All. (He ate the *whole* pie by himself.) |
| **principal** | The person in charge of a school; note the word *pal* in this word. (The *principal* is your *pal*.) |
| **principle** | Rule or standard. (One of the first *principles* in your life should be honesty.) |
| **passed** | Past tense of *pass*. (One quarterback *passed* the ball.) |
| **past** | Happening before. (The sixth grade is in the *past*.) |
| **sense** | Intelligence. (She had enough *sense* to study for the test.) |
| **since** | Dating from a certain time. (That hasn't happened *since* we told him not to ride his motorcycle in the hallways.) |
| **peace** | A calm period. (The war was over, and the two countries were at *peace*.) |
| **piece** | A bit of something. (He tore a *piece* of paper from his notebook.) |
| **are** | To be. (We *are* number one.) |
| **our** | Belonging to us. (That is *our* school on the hill.) |

Here are some other words that many people misspell.

| | |
|---|---|
| **all right** | Everything is okay; correct. Never "alright." Would you write "alwrong" for "all wrong"? (After being sick, Gloria is now *all right*.) |
| **separate** | Move apart. Remember, sep-A-rate. (We had to *separate* the yolks from the whites of these eggs.) |
| **grammar** | What you study in English. Remember, there are only A's in grammar. (The study of *grammar* is useful in all languages.) |
| **I'm** | This means "I am." (*I'm* really happy today.) |
| **library** | A place for books. Don't forget the *r* after the *b*. (Our *library* has some great books.) |
| **receive** | *I* before *e* except after *c* or followed by *g*. (Did you *receive* the letter, yet?) |
| **though** | However; nevertheless. (*Though* he was only 14, he had a license to drive.) |
| **thought** | Past tense of *think*. (He *thought* a lot about his home back in Iowa.) |
| **tough** | Rough. (That bully is really *tough*.) |

**beginning** The start of something. Note: three *n*'s. (Write your name at the beginning of this assignment.)

**sophomore** A tenth grader. Remember, the *o* after the *h*. (The *sophomore* class won the competition yell.)

Directions: In the blank, write the correct spelling of the homonym.

_____    1. She is (all ready, already) driving a car.

_____    2. The answer to that problem can (vary, very) greatly.

_____    3. If you see a misspelled word, (right, write) it correctly in the blank.

_____    4. He wants to (by, bye, buy) a new car with the money he's saved.

_____    5. The dog wagged (its, it's) tail.

_____    6. The class thought that they (new, knew) the answer.

_____    7. Didn't she (here, hear) the question?

_____    8. (Lets, Let's) all gather at the park.

_____    9. (Were, We're) not the ones who cheated.

_____    10. I don't now (wear, where) he is.

_____    11. The (brakes, breaks) on his car went out.

_____    12. They drove down a crooked (road, rode) in San Francisco.

_____    13. English is may favorite (coarse, course).

_____    14. He didn't know (weather, whether) or not to go.

_____    15. He couldn't believe that he ate the (hole, whole) thing.

_____    16. She had to go see the (principal, principle) for her report.

_____    17. The entire class (passed, past) the test.

_____    18. She had a lot of (sense, since).

_____    19. The President wanted (peace, piece) in the Middle East.

_____    20. That is (are, our) car parked over there.

# Spelling Quiz #2

Directions: Circle the correct answer

1. We are (already, all ready) for the long trip ahead.

2. Please choose the (right, write) answer for that question.

3. The results of the two tests didn't (vary, very) at all.

4. When she gets mad, she becomes (vary, very) red in the face.

5. Carson High's football team has (already, all ready) won three games.

6. Did you (right, write) a note to Uncle Harvey?

7. I want to (by, bye, buy) a new radio.

8. The huge boat looked majestic with (its, it's) sails unfurled.

9. She shouted, "(By, Bye, Buy)," as the train pulled away from the depot.

10. (Its, It's) only fair that everyone should get a chance to read.

11. Everyday she had to walk (by, bye, buy) the old, haunted house.

12. Can you (here, hear) me in the back of the room?

13. Jane shouted, "(Lets, Let's) get out of this place!"

14. After he did a lot of research, he (new, knew) the answer to the mystery.

15. The (new, knew) findings have proven that smoking is hazardous to your health.

16. Father (lets, let's) the children go to the movies every Saturday.

17. We saw two snakes right (here, hear) last week.

18. What blouse did you (wear, where) to school yesterday?

19. It seems that plastic sometimes (brakes, breaks) more easily than glass.

20. Where (were, we're) you yesterday?

21. The (brakes, breaks) on her car need repair.

22. (Were, We're) leaving tomorrow for Bakersfield.

23. Does she know (wear, where) to meet us?

24. Try to keep the car on the (road, rode).

25. English is sometimes a tough (coarse, course).

26. She (road, rode) her horse through the woods.

27. This wood feels very (coarse, course).

28. You must learn the (principal, principle) of good behavior.

29. She didn't know (weather, whether) or not to go to the dance.

30. The lion fell into the (hole, whole) that the natives had dug.

31. Sometimes, the (weather, whether) on Mt. Shasta can be fierce.

32. He put his (hole, whole) head through the crack in the fence.

33. The (principal, principle) gave a speech at the assembly.

34. On our trip, we (passed, past) the Grand Canyon.

35. (Sense, Since) he left, the farm has lost money.

36. There was no need to bring a salad (sense, since) three other people had brought one.

37. The Civil War is (passed, past) history.

38. I wish that you would come over to (are, our) house.

39. We're all glad that there is finally (peace, piece) in the world.

40. He had a huge (peace, piece) of cake.

41. What (are, our) you going to do this weekend?

Directions: All eleven of the words from the previous list are in the puzzle below. By reading down and across, you can locate them. Circle them when you find them. One word appears twice.

```
E D W O M A N R T Y M K S S R R U F
O Q U T Y S D F G G X L E D F F E J
I B E G I N N I N G D W P W W O O L
S I F J H K L O P R D C A B V C O B
O K R T I E B X Z Z S A R D S I L S
B E H A D E S F V L M K A N N Z I R
A S O P H O M O R E G O T H O U B O
C I G S D Q G W O M E N R T T T R I
A G I M O I R E C E I V E H O H A O
S U R J D E A W O M A N S O U O R S
E R L E E A M H G R D S A U G U Y S
O T S A X E M K M U I O F G H G D O
I S E Q U D A B Z P O O P H X H E N
A C A L L   R I G H T O P T O I L S
```

You've heard all these words many times. More important, you use them continuously in your writing. Here are some hints that will help you learn to spell them.

| | |
|---|---|
| counselor | The people who plan your classes in school are counselors. (The *counselor* thought I should take more math classes.) |
| judgment | Drop the *e* before adding "ment." (In his *judgment*, the man was guilty.) |
| argument | Drop the *e* before adding "ment." (There's no *argument* about which team is better.) |
| college | This word has two *e*'s. (After high school, Zondra wants to go to *college*. |
| ache | A pain to spell. (He has an ache in his lower back.) |
| clothes | Don't forget the *e* before the *s*. (In PE, we wear gym *clothes*.) |
| education | Learning. (Her high school *education* was very important to her.) |
| embarrass | To make someone feel bad. (She *embarrassed* him in front of his friends.) |
| cause | The reason for an occurrence. This word is a noun. Don't use it when you mean *because*. (The *cause* of the accident was the slippery road.) |
| because | This word is an adverb. Us it to complete a thought. This word answers *why*. (He did it *because* he didn't know any better.) |
| knowledge | Note the *d*. (His *knowledge* of ancient history was astounding.) |
| interest | Note the *e* between the *t* and the *r*. (His *interest* lies totally in sports.) |
| literature | You'll use this word all year when reading books. (She reads a lot in her *literature* class.) |
| license | You'll need one to drive a car. (His driver's *license* has expired.) |
| necessary | Note: One *c*, two *s*'s. (It is *necessary* to pass English to graduate.) |
| probably | This word has three syllables; don't miss the middle one. (She will *probably* go to the dance alone.) |
| quit | To stop. Ends with *it*. (He *quit* his job.) |

| | |
|---|---|
| **quiet** | To make no noise. (It is necessary to be *quiet* in the library so others won't be disturbed.) |
| **quite** | Often confused with *quiet*. (He is *quite* tall for his age.) |
| **sincerely** | Remember the second *e*. (She was *sincerely* thankful for your help.) |
| **studying** | Keep the *y*. (Sally is *studying* for her final exams.) |
| **usually** | Two *u*'s, two *l*'s. (Tom is *usually* here on time.) |
| **writing** | One t. (*Writing* notes in class is against the rules.) |
| **lose** | This is what happens if you don't win. (I hope you don't *lose* that game.) |
| **loose** | Even double *o*'s can't make this word tight. (This knot is too *loose*.) |
| **loss** | Something you suffer. (We suffered a great *loss* when our tropical fish died.) |
| **than** | A comparison. (Joe is taller *than* John.) |
| **then** | A time passed. (He left *then*, he returned.) |
| **assignment** | Don't forget the *g*. (Your *assignment* today is to read Poe's "Raven.") |
| **straight** | The middle of this word is the toughest part to keep *straight*. Remember, "aig." (She drove *straight* home.) |
| **believe** | Remember the *ie*. (*Believe* me when I tell you this.) |
| **business** | Put the accent on the first syllable. (He opened a dry cleaning *business* on Market Street.) |

Directions: In the following essay, fill in the blank that corresponds with the number with the appropriate word from the previous list of thirty-two words and be sure it's spelled correctly. You may use a word more than once, but you must each word at least once.

1. _____

2. _____

3. _____

4. _____

5. _____

6. _____

7. _____

8. _____

9. _____

10. _____

11. _____

12. _____

13. _____

14. _____

15. _____

16. _____

17. _____

18. _____

19. _____

20. _____

My goal in life is simple. After I finish high school, *1* I want to go on to *2* to receive a higher *3*. When I finish there, I want to open a small *4*, selling fine *5* to rich people. I *6* hope to become wealthier *7* anyone in my family before me.

While in high school, I want to gain enough *8* to earn a scholarship to a good *9*. My *10*, Miss Sagehen, advised me to do each *11* in all my classes, use good *12* in the years to come, keep *13* hard, and I will, indeed, acquire a good *14*. There's no *15* with her logic there. I *16* she's *17* right.

I know that I can't afford to *18* any credits, especially in English. Reading works of *19* and *20* skills are two areas in that subject that I find *21* important. I *22* maintain a high level of *23* in English *24* of that.

A *25* of credits can *26* a great deal of heart *27* for students and can *28* you, too. In fact, some students feel so bad about losing credits that they *29* school altogether. That's not good *30* on their part. It is *31* to stay in school if you want to succeed in life. You don't need to get *32* A's either, to succeed, but just try your best.

In order to acquire a *33* *34*, which will allow me to buy at wholesale and sell at retail, I'll need at least two years of training at a junior *35*. There, I'll also learn how to keep books and run a tight ship, so to speak, rather than a *36* organization where I might *37* money.

A lot of people may not *38* in me now, but I'm going to *39* the critics and be a success in selling fine clothing.

21. _____

22. _____

23. _____

24. _____

25. _____

26. _____

27. _____

28. _____

29. _____

30. _____

31. _____

32. _____

33. _____

34. _____

35. _____

36. _____

37. _____

38. _____

39. _____

# Spelling Quiz #3

Directions: Circle the correct spelling of each word.

1. He needed to see his (councilor, counselor) for a program change.

2. The principal needed more facts before she could make a (judgment, judgement).

3. His father did not want an (argument, arguement) about studying with the television off.

4. A (collage, college) degree will open many doors in the future.

5. The overweight man had a tremendous (ache, acke) in his lower back.

6. When skiing, it is necessary to wear the proper (cloths, clothes) to keep warm.

7. A good (education, edjucation) is worth its weight in gold.

8. I hope you don't (embarass, embarrass) your brother tonight.

9. What was the (cause, coz) of the accident.

10. They took umbrellas (because, cause) the weather forecast had predicted rain.

11. Mary has acquired a tremendous amount of (knowlege, knowledge) about the assassination of Lincoln.

12. It helps to find where your occupational (intrest, **interest**) lies before looking for a job.

13. In my (litrature, **literature**) class we're reading *Tom Sawyer*.

14. When I'm sixteen, I'll get my driver's (**license**, lisense).

15. It is (necesary, **necessary**) to do well in school to survive in the job market later on.

16. He is (probly, **probably**) going to try for a field goal.

17. If you (**quit**, quite) too early, you'll never finish.

18. While others are taking a test, it is polite to be (**quiet**, quite).

19. These trigonometry problems seem (quiet, **quite**) hard.

20. The little girl was (sincerly, **sincerely**) grateful for your help.

21. Sally is in her room (studing, **studying**) her algebra.

22. Algernon is (usualy, **usually**) the first one to the bus stop.

23. Kareem Abduhl Amani is (**writing**, writting) a letter to his cousin in Florida.

24. The (lose, **loss**) of her uncle was very traumatic to the young girl.

25. The Falcons can't afford to (**lose**, loose) another game.

26. The lion has broken (lose, **loose**) from its cage.

27. I had to wait longer (**than**, then) I had anticipated.

28. He opened the door, (than, **then**) he pushed his head in first.

29. Have you done the (assinement, **assignment**) in English?

30. She has trouble drawing a (strate, **straight**) line.

31. If you (belive, **believe**, beleive) hard enough, your dreams will come true.

32. What (busness, **business**) is your mother in?

# 10 Prefixes, Roots, and Suffixes

Many words in our language are made up of parts of words from other languages. Latin and Greek have contributed many prefixes, roots words, and suffixes. The longest word in our language is made up of many prefixes, roots, and suffixes: *pneumonoultramicroscopicsilicovolcanocconiosis.*

*pneu* = air
*mono* = one
*ultra* = extreme
*micro* = small
*scop* = see
*ic* = pertaining to
*silico* = sand
*volcano* = an eruption of a mountain
*coni* = dust
*osis* = condition of (usually pertaining to a disease)

This word means a lung disease caused by extremely small dust from the sand of a mountain that had erupted.

The following table will provide you with many prefixes, root words, and suffixes. You can use it for the exercises that follow the table.

## Table of Affixes and Roots

| Prefix | Meaning | Example |
|---|---|---|
| a-, an- | not, without | atypical, anarchy |
| ab- | away, from, off from, away | abdicate |
| ad-, an- | to, toward | admit |
| amib- | both | ambivalence |
| amphi- | both, around, about | amphitheater |
| ana- | up, backward, excessively | anachronism |
| ante- | before, preceding, prior to | antecedent |
| anti- | against | antipathy |
| auto- | self | automobile |
| be- | completely | bedecked |
| by- | near, secondary, incidental | bypath |
| cata-, cath- | down, against, in accordance | catalogued |
| circum | around | circumspect |
| com-, con-, cor-, co- | together with | correlate |
| contra- | against | contradict |

| | | |
|---|---|---|
| de- | down, from, away, out of | depose |
| dia- | through, across, between | diameter |
| dis- | apart from, reversing | dissuade |
| ec-, ex- | out of | exodus, exit |
| en- | in | enamored |
| epi- | upon, beside, among, over | epigram |
| eu- | well, good | eulogy |
| ex- | out of, beyond, without thoroughly, formerly | ex-governor |
| fore- | in front of (position, time) | forecast |
| hyper- | over | hypersensitive |
| hypo- | under, beneath | hypodermic |
| in-, in-, il-, ir- | into, not (as an adjective) | infuse, irrevocable |
| inter-, intro-, intra | between, among, together, within | introduce |
| meta- | with, after, over, beyond | metamorphosis |
| mis- | wrong, wrongly | misinterpret |
| miso- | hatred of | misogynist |
| ob-, oc-, of-, op- | toward, to, against, upon | oppose, obdurate |
| omni- | all | omnibus |
| pan- | all | panacea |
| para- | beside, beyond | paragraph |
| per- | throughout, completely | permit |
| peri- | around | periscope |
| poly- | many | polychrome |
| post- | after | postponed |
| pre- | before | preview |
| pro- | forward | proceed |
| re- | back, again | reduce |
| se- | aside | secede |
| sub-, suc-, suf-, sug-, sup, sus- | under, subordinate | subterranean |
| super- | over, above, above in position | supercilious |
| syn-, sy-, sym- | with, along with, at the same time | synchronize, sympathy |
| trans- | across, beyond | transit |
| vice- | in place of | viceroy |
| with- | against, away | withstand |

# Numbers

| | | |
|---|---|---|
| uni-, mono- | one | unilateral, monogram |
| bi-, di- | two | bicuspid, dialogue |
| tri- | three | tricycle |
| quadra-, tetra | four | quadruped, tetrameter |
| penta-, quin- | five | pentagon, quintuplet |
| sex-, hexa- | six | sextant, hexagon |
| sept-, hepta- | seven | September, heptagon |
| oct- | eight | octave |

| | | |
|---|---|---|
| nona- | nine | nonagenarian |
| dec- | ten | decimate |
| centi- | one hundred | centigrade |
| milli- | one thousand | millennium |
| kilo- | one thousand | kilocycle |
| multi- | many | multigraph |
| semi-, hemi- | half or partially half | semiweekly, hemisphere |

# Common Roots (Latin)

| Latin Root | Meaning | Example |
|---|---|---|
| ag-, -act-, -ig- | move, do | agitate, actuate, exigency |
| -agri- | field | agriculture, agricologist |
| audi-, audit- | hear | audible, auditorium |
| -avi- | bird | aviary, aviation |
| -capit- | heard | capitulate, capitalize |
| -ced-, -cess | move, yield | recede, proceed, secede |
| -cern-, -crete- | distinguish | discern, concern, discrete |
| -cit- | rouse or call | incite, cite |
| -clam- | call, cry out | clamor, declaim |
| -clar- | clear | clarion, clarify |
| -clin- | lean | decline, incline |
| -clud-, -claud-, -clus- | shut | seclude, clause, claustrophobia |
| -cord- | heart | accord, cordial |
| -corp- | body | corpse, corporal |
| -cred- | to believe | credible, credence |
| -crese-, -cret- | grown, rise | crescendo, secretion |
| -curr-, -curs- | run | current, cursive |
| -dic-, dict- | say | dictaphone, dictate, predict |
| -domin- | master | dominion, dominate |
| -duc-, -duct- | lead | conduct, ductile |
| -fac-, -fic-, -fact-, -fect- | to make, do | fact, factory, beneficent |
| -facil- | easy | facile, facility |
| -fer- | bear, carry | transfer, offer |
| -fid- | faith | fidelity, confidential |
| -fin- | end | finally, finish |
| -flect-, -flex- | bend | deflect |
| -fort- | strong | fortitude, discomfort |
| -gen- | race | genteel, progenitor |
| -jac-, -ject- | hurl or throw | projectile, javelin, eject |
| -jun-, -junct- | join | adjunct, junction |
| -laud-, -laudat- | praise | applause |
| -leg-, -lect- | gather, choose, read | lecture, collect, elect legible |
| -legis-, -lex- | law | legal, legislature |
| -loqu-, -locut- | speak | loquacious, elocution |
| -lux-, -luc- | light | lucidity, elucidate |
| -magn- | great | magnificent, magnanimous |
| -mal- | bad | malevolent, malediction |
| -man- | hand | manipulate, manual |

| | | |
|---|---|---|
| -mit-, -miss- | send | transmit, missile |
| -mov-, -mot- | set in motion | mobile, move, motor |
| -nov-, novus | new | novel, renovation |
| -offic- | duty | official, officer |
| -pac- | peace | pacify, pacific |
| -pel-, -puls- | urge, drive | propel, expulsion |
| -pend-, pens | hang, weigh | pendant, pensive |
| -pet- | seek, ask | petition, repeat |
| -plen- | full | plenty, replenish |
| -plic-, -plex- | bend, fold | Plexiglas, duplicate |
| -pon-, -pos- | place, put | oppose, postpone |
| -salu- | healthy | salutary, salubrious |
| -sci- | know | conscience, science |
| -scrib-, -script- | write | describe, ascribe |
| -sed-, -sess- | set | sedentary, session |
| -sen- | old | senile, senior |
| -sent-, sens- | feel | sentiment, sensitive |
| -seque-, -secut- | follow | sequence, persecute |
| -solv-, -solut- | loosen | solvent, solution |
| -spec-, -spect- | look | spectator, specimen |
| -spir-, spirit- | breath | expire, inspire |
| -sta- | stand firm | stable, stationary |
| -stru-, struct- | build | construe, instruct, construct |
| -sum-, -sumpt- | spend, take up | consume, presume |
| -tect- | cover | protect, detective |
| -ten- | hold | tenacious, tentacle |
| -tend-, tens- | stretch | extend, tendency, tension |
| -tort- | to twist | distort, extort |
| -tract- | draw | tractor, extract |
| -ven-, -vent | come | convene, venture, convention |
| -ver- | true | verily, veritable |
| -vert-, vers- | turn | vertical, converse, reverse |
| -vinc-, -vict- | conquer | convince, victory |
| -viv-, -vit- | live, life | vivacious, survive, vitality |
| -vid-, -vis- | see | evident, provision |
| -voc- | call | vocation, invoke |
| -vol- | wish | voluntary, volition |

# Common Roots (Greek)

| Root | Meaning | Example |
|---|---|---|
| -anthrop- | man | anthropology, philanthropy |
| -arch- | first, chief | monarch, archbishop |
| -aster- | star | astrology, asterisk |
| -bibl- | book | Bible, bibliography |
| -bio | life | biography, biology |
| -chrom- | color | chromatic, Kodachrome |
| -chron- | time | chronometer, chronological |
| -crypt- | secret | cryptic, cryptogram |

| | | |
|---|---|---|
| -dem- | people | democracy, epidemic |
| -derm- | skin | dermatology, epidermis |
| -dox- | opinion | orthodox, paradox |
| -gam- | marriage | polygamy, misogamy |
| -gen- | birth | progeny, eugenics |
| -geo- | earth | geopolitics, geography |
| -gyn- | woman | gynecology, misogynist |
| -graph-, -gram- | write, written something, written | photograph, monogram, program |
| -hetero- | different | heterogeneous, heterdox |
| -homo- | same | homogeneous, homologous |
| -hydr- | water | hydrometer, hydrate |
| -lith- | stone | lithography, monolith |
| -log-, -logy- | speech, word, study of | catalogue, astrology |
| -mega- | great | megacephalic, megalomania |
| -meter, -metr | measure | metronome, thermometer |
| -micro- | small | microscope, microphone |
| -nom-, nomy- | law | economy, astronomy |
| -path- | feeling, suffering | sympathy, psychopathy |
| -phan- | show | diaphanous, cellophane |
| -phil- | love | philologist, philosopher |
| -phon- | sound | phonetics, dictaphone |
| -photo- | light | photogenic, photograph |
| -physio- | nature | physiology, physics |
| -pod- | foot | chriopody, tripod |
| -polis- | city | metropolis, political |
| -psych- | mind | psychology, psychic |
| -pyr- | fire | pyromaniac, pyre |
| -scop- | see | stethoscope, microscope |
| -soph- | wise | philosopher, sophistry |
| -tele- | far | telegraphy, telescope |
| -the- | god | atheist, pantheism |
| -tom- | cut | epitome, anatomy |
| -trop- | turning | heliotrope, tropic, tropism |
| -zo- | animal | zodiac, zoology |

# Suffixes

| Suffix | Meaning | Example |
|---|---|---|
| -able, -ible, -ble | capable of, worthy of | noticeable, voluble |
| -acious, -cious | tending to, or have the quality of | pugnacious, capacious |
| -acy, -cy | state of being, or quality | accuracy, hesitancy |
| -age | state of | marriage, hostage |
| -al | pertaining to | marital, casual |
| -an, -ian | designating or belong to | artesian, guardian |
| -ance, -ancy | state, quality, act or condition | persistence, brilliance agency, vacancy |
| -ant, -ent | one who acts | registrant, student |

| | | |
|---|---|---|
| -ar, -er, -or | one who acts | bursar, teacher, doctor |
| -ard, -art | one who acts ignominiously or does something excessively | braggart, drunkard, coward |
| -ful | full of, abounding in | cheerful, masterful |
| -fy, -efy, -ify | to make | defy, rarefy, testify |
| -hood | state of | childhood, neighborhood |
| -ic, ical | of, pertaining to, similar or like | moronic, historic, historical |
| -ice | act, quality, or state | justice, cowardice |
| -ile, -il | pertaining to, like | servile, civil |
| -ine (fem.) | one who acts | heroine |
| -ion | state or condition of | dominion, tension |
| -ish | state, condition or acting like, in the nature of, or similar to | implish, selfish, mannish |
| -ar, -ary | pertaining to, connected with | secular, elementary |
| -ate, -ite | possessing or being | favorite, incapacitates |
| -cle, -cule | diminutives | particle, molecule |
| -dom | a state or condition | martyrdom, serfdom |
| -eer, -ier | one who acts | furrier, auctioneer |
| -en | made of, to make of suggesting smallness | leaden, lessen, |
| -ent, -ens | doing, behaving, existing | apparent, reverent, subsequent |
| -ette | small or dimunitive | dinette, statuette |
| -ess, -trix (fem.) | one who acts | waitress, aviatrix |
| -ese | of, or relating to | journalese |
| -esque | in the manner of | picturesque, grotesque |
| -ferous | bringing, yielding | odoriferous, carboniferous |
| -ific, -fix | making or causing | pacific, soporific |
| -ism | art of, philosophy of, practice of | liberalism, Americanism |
| -ist | one who acts | philanthropist, atheist |
| -ity, -ty | condition, state or degree of | gratuity, plenty |
| -ive | having the nature of, giving of tending toward | imaginative, collective |
| -ize, -ise | to make into, to practice | mesmerize, familiarize |
| -le, -el | diminutiveness | teakettle, icicle |
| -lent, -ulent | abounding in | violent, fraudulent |
| -less | without, beyond the limit | fearless, useless |
| -ly | similar in manner | dearly, fully, carefully |
| -ment | state, quality, or act of | detriment, entanglement |
| -mony | abstract condition | acrimony, ceremony |
| -ness | state or condition | strictness, fairness |
| -ory | of, pertaining to place of, or for | auditory, prohibitory, offertory . |
| -ose, -ous | state or quality of | comatose, furious |
| -ship | state or quality, art or skill | courtship, partnership |
| -some | like or same | bothersome, quarrelsome |
| -ster (masculine) | one who acts | pollster |
| -stress (feminine) | one who acts | songstress |
| -try | art or profession of | forestry, ministry |
| -tude | state or quality | platitude, aptitude |
| -ure | act or process, result of | adventure, tenure |

Directions: Using the tables of affixes and roots, define the following parts of the words below. Then, unscramble the definition and write out a usable definition.

Example: telephone = tele = far
                          vis  = see
                          ion  = condition of
       television = condition of seeing far

1. microbiology

2. procedure

3. antipathy

4. repel

5. impossible

6. malcontent

7. monogram

8. postponed

9. pacify

10. fortify

11. senseless

12. construct

3. vocal

14. geography

15. subtract

Directions: Using the tables of affixes and roots, define the following words.

1. psychology

2. photograph

3. polygamy

4. preface

5. lecture

6. invincible

7. solution

8. distort

9. pensive

10. chronometer

11. sympathy

12. telephone

13. tripod

14. pantheism

15. philosophy

# 11 Using the Dictionary

There are two kinds of dictionaries: *abridged* and *unabridged*. An abridged dictionary is not as detailed as an unabridged dictionary. It doesn't contain as many words nor give as much information on each word as an unabridged dictionary does. An unabridged dictionary contains all words and give definitions in great detail.

You can use a dictionary for several functions besides finding the definition or spelling of a word. A dictionary will help you with compound words, comparatives and superlatives, syllabication, preferred spelling, verb tenses, synonyms, plurals, etymology, and more.

Directions: From the two paragraphs above, fill in the blanks below.

_____

_____

_____

_____

_____

_____

_____

_____

_____

_____

_____

_____

1. There are _____ kinds of dictionaries: _____ and _____ .

2. An abridged dictionary is not as _____ as an unabridged dictionary.

3. You'll find all words in a(n) _____ dictionary.

4. A dictionary will help you with _____ _____ , _____ and _____ , _____ , _____ _____ , verb tenses, synonyms, and _____ , _____ , and more.

## Guide Words

The two words at the top of each page of a dictionary are called guide words. The word on the left is the first word on the page. The word on the right is the last word on the page.

Directions: Use your dictionary to find the guide words for the following words:

_____

_____

1. eclipse

_____   2. obvious

_____

# Preferred Spelling

The spelling that is considered to be better is called the preferred spelling. Both spellings of the words are *correct*. One spelling is preferred. There are two ways that dictionaries list preferred spelling:

  1. when side-by-side, the first word
  2. the word without British spelling

Directions: Use your dictionary to write what the preferred spelling of the following words is.

_____   1. theater, theatre

_____   2. catalogue, catalog

_____   3. judgement, judgment

_____   4. axe, ax

_____   5. neighbour, neighbor

# Syllabication

A syllable is a group of letters that makes a single sound. In a dictionary, syllables are generally divided by dots: gram·mar, sep·a·rate.

When you come to the end of a line while writing, you may have to divide a word into syllables. For example, if you were to divide the word *grammar* at the end of a line, you'd have to divide it between the m's. Note this example:

> *In English we*
> *are studying gram-*
> *mar.*

There are three rules you must remember:
1. Always divide a word only where the syllable breaks;
2. Never divide a one-syllable word;
3. Never divide a word so that a one-letter syllable is stranded by itself. If you divided *about*, you'd leave the *a* by itself.

Directions: Where do the following words break into syllables? If a word can be divided at the end of a line by the margin, write *yes* after it. If it can't, write *no*.

| Example: | Syllables | Can this word be divided? |
|---|---|---|
| highway | high way | yes |
| about | a bout | no |
| talk | talk | no |
| 1. beautiful | _____ | _____ |
| 2. correct | _____ | _____ |
| 3. enough | _____ | _____ |

4. twelve   _____   _____

5. always   _____   _____

# Compound Words

A compound word is a word that is made up of two or more other words. It is either one word (drugstore), two words (half brother), or a hyphenated word (quarter-hour). If you can't find a word written as one word or a hyphenated word in a dictionary, then assume the compound is two words.

Directions: Use your dictionary to decide if the following words should be one word, two words, or a hyphenated word.

1. allright   _____   (Hint: spell allwrong correctly)

2. a lot   _____

3. makeup   _____   (Meaning the way something is put

together; composition")

4. locker room   _____

5. log book   _____

# Foreign Words

English has words from many foreign languages. Over hundreds of years, we've borrowed words from many languages. We've used some so long that they've become ours. On the other hand, we use some words that are still considered foreign. An example is *adiós*. Words like this are called *foreign*. If we've used the word long enough to make it ours, it's called *anglicized*. Some dictionaries have an entire section called "Foreign Words and Phrases."

Directions: Use your dictionary to decide if these words are foreign or anglicized. Put an X by the following words if they're foreign.

1. matinee   _____   3. debonair   _____

2. status (in) quo _____   4. tempus fugit _____

# Pronounciation

Dictionaries give you the pronounciation of a word right after the word: complex (kəm-pleks). *Then, on the bottom of every odd-numbered page*, you're told how to pronounce the vowels and the blends. In complex (kəm-pleks), the ə is called a schwa and is pronounced like both the *a* and the *u* in the word *abut*.

Directions: Use your dictionary and the pronunciation of the following words. Be prepared to pronounce them.

1. preferable   _____

2. genuine   _____

3. mischievous   _____

# Etymology

Etymology is the study of words and where they come from. Usually, the original meaning (the first meaning) of a word is listed first; for example, slogan {orig. A Scottish war cry}. The word *Orig.* means original or the word's first meaning.

Directions: Use your dictionary and write the original or first meanings of the following words.

1. bedlam      _____

2. dunce      _____

A dictionary also tells you the language from which we get a word. The name of the language is generally abbreviated. There's a table of abbreviations in the front of the dictionary. For example, you'll see this kind of entry: goose {ME<OE<OHG}. The < sign means derived from. The first language listed is the one from which the word comes. If you looked at the table of abbreviations, you'd see that the word *goose* comes from Middle English. It came to Middle English from Old English from Old High German.

Directions: Use your dictionary and write the language from which the following words come. (Do not abbreviate).

1. salad      _____

2. dispute      _____

# Synonyms

Synonyms are words that mean the same thing or about the same thing as the word you're looking up. Dictionaries usually give you a list of these words and label them "synonyms" or "syn."

Directions: Use your dictionary to name synonyms of the following words:

1. advice      _____

2. freedom      _____

# Tenses

Every verb has tenses: present, past, past participle, and present participle.

Example: teach

| Present | Past | Past Participle | Present Participle |
|---------|------|-----------------|--------------------|
| teach | taught | taught | teaching |

The tenses are listed in that order in a dictionary.

Directions: Use your dictionary to look up the tenses of the following words:

| | Present | Past | Past Participle | Present Participle |
|---|---------|------|-----------------|--------------------|
| 1. | swim | _____ | _____ | _____ |
| 2. | eat | _____ | _____ | _____ |

# Plurals

Plural means more than one. A dictionary will indicate the plural of a word with the symbol "pl." Most dictionaries give you the plural by respelling the last syllable: cactus- {pl. *uses, ti*}. So the plurals of *cactus* are *cactuses* and *cacti*. If plural is given, simply add *s*.

Directions: Use your dictionary to find the plurals of the following words.

1. book _____

2. deer _____

3. father-in-law _____

4. crisis _____

5. index _____

# Comparative and Superlative

Use a comparative for two; use a superlative for three or more.

Example: comparative: *tall — taller*.
superlative: *tall — taller — tallest*.

One person is *tall*, the second is *taller*, the third is the *tallest*, the fourth, fifth, one hundredth would be the *tallest*.

As in the example, use *-er* for comparative and *-est* for superlative. Sometimes you must use *more* for comparative and *most* for superlative.

Example: She is *more* beautiful than the other girl.
She is the *most* beautiful girl in the school.

Never use both *more* and *er* or *most* and *est*.

Example: most healthy or healthiest, never most healthiest

Directions: Write the comparative and superlative of the following words. They're listed in the dictionary right after the word. Sometimes the spelling will change: much — *more* (comparative) — *most* (superlative). If nothing is listed *-er* and *-est* for single syllable words and *more* and *most* for words of two or more syllables.

|  | Word | Comparative | Superlative |
|---|---|---|---|
| Example: | big | bigger | biggest |
| 1. | ill | _____ | _____ |
| 2. | bad | _____ | _____ |
| 3. | good | _____ | _____ |
| 4. | handsome | _____ | _____ |
| 5. | pretty | _____ | _____ |

# Parts of Speech

A dictionary also lists parts of speech. Abbreviations are explained in the front of the dictionary. The part of speech is listed after the pronunciation; *complex (kəm-pleks) adj.* Sometimes a word can be more than one part of speech.

Directions: Use your dictionary to name the part(s) of speech of the following.

1. ugly _____

2. leap _____

3. but _____

# Capitals

Words may have different meanings when they're capitalized. For example, *catholic* means "universal," while *Catholic* means "a member of the church of that same name." Some dictionaries list the small lettered word and the capitalized word separately. Most dictionaries do something like this: catholic-1. universal; 2. [C] a member of the church of that same name. Note the capital *C* in the brackets after the number two.

Directions: Use your dictionary to give the meaning for the following they're written with a small letter *and* a capital.

1. congress

   Congress

2. god

   God

# Labels

Some words have labels. The dictionary will give you these labels in the definition. Here are some common labels:

> *archaic* — the word is old-fashioned (mayhap)
> *colloquial* — the word is more suited for informal rather than formal use (boss)
> *obsolete* — the word is too old to be used anymore (gantelope)
> *slang* — the word is substandard and used in certain groups only (stoner)

Directions: Use your dictionary to find the labels of the following words.

1. saith          _____

2. lu lu          _____

# Appendix

A variety of information can be found in the appendix at the back of the dictionary.

Directions: Use the appendix to answer the following questions:

1. Give the words for these abbreviations:

   sfc.          _____

pcs. _____

LZ _____

oz. _____

2. Which biology sign or symbol is used for tree or shrub? _____

3. Who is Booker T. Washington? _____

4. How high is Mt. Hood in Oregon? _____

5. When was Victor Valley College begun? _____

6 What salutation in a letter would you see if you were writing a letter to the Pope? _____ _____

7. What does your name mean? _____

# Review

1. Name the two ways dictionaries list preferred spelling.

    a. _____

    b. _____

2. Why can't you split a word like alone at the end of a line? _____

3. Compound means _____ or more.

4. If we've used a word in our languages so long that it becomes ours, that word is not foreign but _____ _____ .

5. What do you call this symbol: ə ? _____

6. The original meaning of a word is listed where in the definition? _____

7. What does this symbol mean < ? _____

8. Present participles end in _____ .

9. Use a comparative for two; use a _____ for three or more.

10. The appendix is located where? _____

11. Where do you find the pronunciation of vowels and blends? _____

12. Where do you find guide words? _____

13. Where must you split a word at the end of a line? _____

14. Words may have _____ meanings when they're capitalized.

15. _____ is the study of words and where they come from.

16. _____ are words that mean the same thing or about the same thing as the word you're looking up.

# 12 Using the Library

The library is a wonderful source of information of all kinds.

## Non-fiction/Fiction Books

In the library, books are arranged on the shelves in two ways. This is based on whether a book is non-fiction (true) or fiction (not true). Fiction is arranged alphabetically by the last name of the author. Non-fiction is arranged by Dewey Decimal numbers. They are put into number ranges by their subjects. In other words, a book on World War II, because it's history, would be found in the 900–999 section.

Here's a list of the Dewey Decimal non-fiction categories:

000–099     General works (encyclopedias, other reference books)
100–199     Philosophy (psychology, conduct, personality)
200–299     Religion
300–399     Social sciences (economics, government, education, law, etiquette, folklore, legends, fairy tales)
400–499     Languages (grammar, foreign languages, dictionaries)
500–599     Science
600–699     Useful arts (home economics, television, engineering, health, aviation)
700–799     Fine arts (painting, motion pictures, sports, recreation)
800–899     Literature (poetry, drama, essays)
900–909     History
910–919     Travel
92          Biographies
Q           Oversize

1. In what Dewey Decimal range would you find the following non-fiction books?

_____     a book about Bigfoot

_____     a book about prisoners of the Vietnam War

_____     a book dealing with verbs and nouns

_____     a book by Robert Frost

_____     a book explaining how to fix Baked Alaska

2. Arrange the following fiction books as you would find them on the shelves of a library. Remember, they're arranged by author's last name.
   *The Old Man and the Sea* by Ernest Hemingway
   *The Red Pony* by John Steinbeck
   *The Sea Around Us* by Rachel Carson

*The Illustrated Man* by the Ray Bradbury
*Dandelion Wine* by Ray Bradbury

Name of book

_____

_____

_____

_____

3. Demonstrate to the teacher that you can locate a non-fiction book by finding one under the subject supplied by the teacher.

Subject _____ Teacher's initial _____

4. Demonstrate to the teacher that you can locate a fiction book by finding the title given to you by the teacher.

Name of Book _____ Teacher's initial _____

# Card Catalog

Every book in the library has three cards for it in the card catalog — a *subject* card, a *title* card, and an *author* card. A book named *Football Fury* by Bob Waterfield has three cards to help you locate the book. One is listed under the author's name, *Waterfield*. One is listed under the title, *Football Fury*. One is listed under the subject, *football*. If a card has a Dewey Decimal number in the upper left-hand corner, it's obviously a non-fiction book. If it has just a letter, then it's a fiction book. Here's an example.

Example:

| 621.35<br>S | | S |
|---|---|---|
| | | |
| Non-fiction | | Fiction |

By the way, many large libraries now use a microfiche card catalog. The information can be found in the same location as it is on the card. Just ask a librarian how to use the machine and you'll be in business.

Directions: In your library, use the card catalog to find the following information.

1. Name any fiction book by each of these authors:

John Steinbeck _____

Jack London _____

2. Who wrote the following fiction books?

*Starman Jones* _____

*Little Women* _____

3. Name a non-fiction book on each of these subjects and give the Dewey Decimal number:

motorcycles _____

photography _____

# Readers' Guide to Periodical Literature

The *Reader's Guide* lists magazine articles written during the period of time printed on the spine and the front cover of that reference book. Always check the date on the front of the *Readers' Guide*.

An article is found two ways in a *Readers' Guide*. It is listed under the author's name and under the subject title. In other words, if you're trying to locate the article "Pac-Man vs. Ms. Pac-Man" by Perry Paclinger, you'd find it listed in two places in the *Readers' Guide* — under *video games* (subject) and under *Paclinger* (author).

When you find the article, here's what you might see:
  VIDEO GAMES
    Pac-Man vs. Ms. Pac-Man. P. Paclinger. U.S. News
      34: 65−6+      Ap 26 '89.

The following information is included in *The Readers' Guide* entry:

1. subject title       – *video games*
2. article title       – *Pac-Man vs. Ms. Pac-Man*
3. author           – *P. Paclinger*
4. name of magazine – *U.S. News*
5. volume number of the magazine – *34*
6. Pages in the magazine – *65–66*
7. continued on other pages – *±*
8. date (April 26, 1989) – *Ap 26 '89*

Directions: Answer the following questions:

1. From the following sample entry, answer the questions below.

   SKIING
   Boots that keep you warm. J. Poma. Skiing
   26:82−3      Ja 7 '86

   volume number     _____

   author          _____

   name of magazine _____

   page number      _____

   date            _____

   article title     _____

   subject title     _____

2. Generally, in the front of the *Readers' Guide*, there is a list of abbreviations. Find it and what tell these abbreviations mean:

il., illus. _____

cond. _____

por. _____

v. _____

Je _____

3. Check out one magazine on a topic of your choice. Show the teacher:

  • the Readers' Guide listing

  • the magazine article

Teacher's initials _____

# Other Reference Books

There are many other sources of information in the library.

Directions: Use the library to find the following information. Show it to your teacher.

Teacher's initials

1. football statistics from an almanac _____

2. a list of national parks from an encyclopedia _____

3. a map of Taiwan from an atlas _____

4. the population of California from an almanac _____

5. a synonym for SPUNK from *Roget's Thesaurus* _____

6. a picture of Picasso's works from an encyclopedia _____

7. an article on Franklin Roosevelt from *Facts About Presidents* _____

8. a short biography of Karl Marx in *Who's Who* _____

9. an article on Ernest Hemingway in *20th Century Authors* _____

10. the quote "To thine own self be true" in *Familiar Quotations* and write down who said this.

Who said it: _____  _____

# Summary

_____

_____

_____

1. All books are either _____ or _____ .

2. Non-fiction books are arranged by _____ .

3. Fiction books are arranged by _____ .

_____

_____

_____

_____

_____

_____

_____

_____

_____

_____

_____

_____

_____

4. There are _____ cards for every book in the library.

5. Those cards are the _____ card, the _____ card, and the _____ card.

6. If a card has a number in the upper left-hand corner, it's a _____ book.

7. If it has a letter only in the upper left-hand corner, it's a _____ book.

8. *Readers' Guides* list _____ written during the period of time printed on the front cover.

9. An article is found in two ways: under the _____ and under the _____ .

10. A list of national parks would be found in an _____ .

11. A short biography of a person would be found in _____ .

12. A map of a city or country would be found in an _____ .

# 13 Writing Business Letters

So far in this text-workbook you have studied English grammar and usage. This unit will teach you write business letters. This is an important skill to have. You might want to request the services of a computer dating service, write to the principal of your school, communicate with a company concerning a defective part on your motorcycle, or contact a company about a job. Whatever the goal, a correctly written business letter will be more successful than one that doesn't follow the rules.

Here are five simple steps to a better business letter:

**Step 1** *Think and decide*   A business letter that gets results has a plan. Think about what you want to accomplish with your letter and then decide what results you want to get. Write these results down in a complete sentence.

>   Example:  The result I want from my letter is to get the defective part on my motorcycle replaced
>             at no cost to me.

**Step 2** *Research*   Keep the purpose of your letter in mind. Your second step is to gather all the background information you will need to include in your letter.

>   Example: a. Get the name and address of the manufacturer of your motorcycle.
>            b. Find out the name and/or number of the defective part. Write down this
>               information on your scratch paper.

**Step 3** *Use a proper business letter form*   The third step is very important. You should always follow proper business letter form. Use semi-block style shown on page    . Your reader will not take an improperly written letter.

**Step 4** *Be brief and clear*   Your letter's purpose should be clear, its sentences short, and its words well chosen. Remember that the person who receives your letter is busy and does not have time to read letters that are too long or say things in a less than courteous way. Your letter should have a brief reading time (the average business letter takes a mere forty-five seconds of reading time).

**Step 5** *Be neat and error-free*   Your fifth and final step is to check your letter for appearance and possible errors in form, spelling, and punctuation. Your letter must be neat, clean and free from errors. In other words, it must be perfect.

Directions: Complete the exercise below by filling in the blanks. The answers are found in the material you have just read.

1. Knowing how to write a business letter is an _____ to have.

2. You might want to request the services of a _____ _____ _____ or write to the _____ of your school about something happening on campus, or perhaps communicate with a company concerning a _____ _____ _____ on your motorcycle.

3. Whatever the _____ , a correctly written business letter will be more successful than one that doesn't follow the rules.

4. The first step is to _____ and _____ what results you want to get.

5. Write these results down in a _____ _____ _____ .

6. Your second step is to gather all the _____ _____ _____ you will need to include in your letter.

7. You should always follow proper business letter for. Use _____ _____ style.

8. Remember that the person who receives your letter is busy and does not have time to read letters that are _____ _____ or say things in a less than _____ way.

9. Your letter's purpose should be _____ , its sentences _____ _____ , and its words _____ _____ _____ .

10. Your fifth and final step is to check your letter for appearance and possible errors in _____ _____ and _____ .

11. In other words, it must be _____ .

Most business letters use semi-block style. That refers to the form of the letter. Here is an example of the semi-block style. The beginning of the paragraphs in semi-block style are indented.

100 North Adams Street
Portland, OR 92361
March 7, 19___

Ms. Rachael Effram
Consumer Information
Scooter World
1000 Ventura Boulevard
Seaside, WA 90000

Dear Ms. Effram

I am interested in the new model 900 Scoot-Toot. Please send me your company's product information brochure and any other literature you have available, Thank you.

Sincerely,

*Tom Beamer*

Tom Beamer

Directions: The six parts of a business letter are listed in the following. Label each example in the preceding letter matching the number of each part with the number shown on the example.

1. heading
2. inside address
3. greeting or salutation
4. body
5. closing
6. signature

Here are some business letter facts. The margins are the spaces on the sides, top, and bottom of your paper. The left margin should be straight and about an inch wide. The right margin can be a little narrower than the left. Center the whole letter on the page with just about the same margin at the top as at the bottom. Write in blue or black ink only, not pencil. A typewritten letter is even better. Use plain (unruled) white paper only. Write on only one side of the paper. If you need two sheets, number the second. Use your neatest writing or printing. Keep your letter clean by being careful when you write. If you make an error, it's better to start over. Fold your letter neatly before putting it into a carefully addressed envelope.

Directions: Answer the following questions about business letters.

1. Most business letters use _____-_____ style.

2. The beginning of paragraphs in this style are _____.

3. The six parts of a business letter are the _____, _____, _____, _____, _____, _____, _____.

4. The _____ are the spaces on the sides, top, and bottom of your paper.

5. Center the whole letter on the page with just about the same margin at the _____ _____ as at the _____.

6. Write in _____ or _____ ink.

7. Use plain (unruled) white _____ only.

8. Write on only one side of the _____ .

9. Use your best _____ or printing.

10. Keep your letter clean by being careful when you _____ .

# Parts of a Business letter

## 1. The Heading

Begin the heading at least an inch from the top of the page. Write your complete address and date in the upper right hand corner of the page. Write the heading without any abbreviation, except for the state name. Always put a comma between the city and state and another one between the day and year.

**Sample heading**

2424 Hilltop Drive

Duluth, MN 37054

May 10, 19__

**Put your own heading here:**

_____

_____

_____

## 2. The Inside Address

The inside address belongs at least two spaces (four, if typed) below the heading, against the left-hand margin. It includes the name and address of the company to which you are writing. Use the same punctuation as the heading. If the name or title of the company representative is known, that should be included in the inside address.

**Sample inside address:**

Crumby Cookie Company

1600 Oreo Street

San Francisco, CA 96087

**Put the address of any company here. Use a telephone directory or make one up.**

_____

_____

_____

## 3. The Greeting

The greeting, or salutation, is placed two spaces below the last line of the inside address, against the left-hand margin. *Dear Sir* or *Dear Madam* is used most often and is always followed by a *colon*. When you know the name of the individual within the business to which you are writing, use his or her title (Mr., Ms., Dr.,) and last name instead of *Dear Madam* or *Dear Sir*.

**Sample greeting:**

Dear Sir:

Dear Madam:

Dear Mr. Johnson:

**Put a greeting here. Don't forget the colon!**

_____

_____

_____

## 4. The Body

The body is the letter itself. If the letter is very short (seven lines or less), you use double-spacing for the entire body of the letter. Normally, you use single-spacing within paragraphs and double-spacing between them.

## 5. The Closing

The closing comes between the body of the letter and the signature. The closing is placed just to the right of the center of the page, two spaces below the last line of the body of your letter. It is followed by a comma.

**Sample closings:**                                      **Put all five closings here. Don't forget the comma!**

Very truly yours,                                         _____

Yours truly,                                              _____

Yours very truly,                                         _____

Sincerely yours,                                          _____

Yours sincerely,                                          _____

## 6. The Signature

Sign your full name, first and last, to your letter. Do not put *Miss*, *Ms.* or *Mr.* before your name. Your signature should always be handwritten. If your letter is typed, type your name four spaces below the closing, directly under the first letter of the closing. Sign your name in the space.

**Sample signature:**                                     **Put your own signature here:**

Greta Gorgeous                                            _____

Directions: Fill in the blanks.

1.  Begin the heading at least an inch from the top of the page. Write your _____ _____ and the date.

2.  Write the heading without _____.

3.  Always put a comma between the _____ and _____ _____ and another one between the day and year.

4.  The inside address belongs at least _____ _____ _____ (four, if typed) below the heading, against the left-hand margin.

5.  It includes the _____ and _____ and the company to which you are writing.

6.  Use the same punctuation as the _____.

7.  The greeting is placed two spaces below the last line of the _____ _____, against the left-hand margin.

8. *Dear Sir,* and *Dear Madam* are used most often and are always followed by a _____ _____.

9. The body is the _____ _____.

10. The closing comes between the body of the letter and the _____.

11. The closing is placed just to the right of the _____ of the page, two spaces below the last line of the body of your letter.

12. It is followed by a _____.

13. Sign your _____ _____, first and last, to your letter.

14. Your signature should always be _____.

Directions: It's time to put these letter-writing skills to work. Select a business from which you are *really interested* in hearing. Here are some ideas: the principal of your school, your favorite TV show, a company offering a free catalog or sample, a group from which you'd like information, a company to ask about a job or order some merchandise, a company to complain or compliment.

Use the following form to plan your letter. When you're satisfied it's perfect, complete your final copy on a separate sheet of paper.

Heading {
_____
_____
_____

_____
_____ } Inside Address
_____

_____ } Greeting or salutation

_____
_____
_____
_____  } Body
_____
_____
_____

Closing { _____

Signature { _____

 # The Writing Process

Many people think they can't write because they can't produce perfect copy on their first try. There are three steps to follow that make producing a successful piece of writing simpler. These steps are *prewriting*, *writing*, and *postwriting*. As you begin writing, slow down and spend time on each step. It will help you organize your ideas. And with practice the steps will go quickly.

Directions: Fill in the blanks, based on the information you've just read.

1.  Many people think they can't _____ because they can't produce a perfect copy on their _____ try.

2.  There are _____ to follow that make producing a successful piece of _____ simpler.

3.  These steps are _____, _____ and ____ _____.

   Prewriting is the first stage in the writing process. If helps you to discover what you have to say about a topic. It is like thinking out loud on paper. The methods of prewriting that you are going to learn in this text-workbook include brainstorming, grouping ideas into categories, and mapping. Brainstorming is an excellent tool for you if your mind goes blank when you are asked to write. In brainstorming you start by thinking about a general topic. Then you quickly jot down any words or phrases that pop into your head. As you write, one idea leads to another. Write down everything you think of whether or not it seems to really fit the topic. After you've practiced, you should be able to brainstorm almost any topic in six minutes or less.

Directions: Fill in the blanks based on what you have just read about prewriting and brainstorming.

1.  _____ is the first stage in the writing process.

2.  The methods of prewriting that you are going to learn in this tex-workbook include _____ _____, grouping ideas into _____, and _____ _____.

3.  In brainstorming you start by thinking about a _____.

4.  Write down everything you _____ of whether or not it seems to really fit the _____.

5.  After you've practiced, you should be able to brainstorm any topic in _____ minutes or less.

What images appear in your mind when you see or hear the word brainstorming? A blizzard of snow? A burst of fireworks? What are your ideas? Quickly jot down the first three images that come to your mind when you think of a brainstorm.

_____

_____

_____

You have just brainstormed! You let your mind go free, without prejudging what came into it. Then you wrote it down. That's brainstorming. You write quickly and judge later. The point is to write something so that you'lll have something to judge. No, let's take a few minutes to practice brainstorming.

Directions: Using one of the general topics listed below, write down anything that comes to mind. Don't worry about having complete sentences or perfect spelling for now. Just jot down words or phrases as qucikly as you can think of them. If you get stuck, here are some hints to get you started:

1. List your feelings (sad, happy, excited,) about the topic.
2. List your experiences (successes, embarrassments,) with it.
3. List what you know (facts, figures,) about it.

cars                                            weekends

clothes                                         junk food

# Categorizing

The next step in prewriting is categorizing, which is putting your brainstorming ideas into groups. Doing this helps you to begin to organize and weed out those ideas that aren't helpful.

Directions: Here is an exercise in categorizing. Each of the twenty words scattered below belongs to one of five different categories or groups. Look over the words carefully. Decide what the five categories are and write them below. Then list the words, four in each category, in the correct column. The first one has been started for you.

eagle   football   Datsun

Chrysler  orange   soccer   bluebird

Ford   watermelon  canary

apple   pen   crayon  banana

owl   baseball   Chevrolet

pencil   magic marker  basketball

Writing Tools _____  _____  _____

_____  _____  _____

_____  _____  _____

_____  _____  _____

_____  _____  _____

_____  _____

_____  _____

_____  _____

_____  _____

*English Made Easy*

Directions: In this exercise, the category names are mixed up with the words that fit into the categories. There are three categories, and each category has four details. The general topic is *sports*. After looking over the words, decide what the three categories are. Then, under each group list the four words that fit into each category.

**Sports**

| | | |
|---|---|---|
| swimming | individuals | bicycling |
| racquetball | soccer | tennis |
| teams | arm wrestling | baseball |
| boxing | partners | running |
| gymnastics | volleyball | basketball |

Categories: _____  _____  _____

_____  _____  _____

_____  _____  _____

_____  _____  _____

_____  _____  _____

Directions: Look back to the exercise where you brainstormed four topics. Look at your brainstorming. If you can think of anything else to add, go ahead and add it now. Next, think of some categories or groups into which some of your brainstormed ideas fit into. The categories may or may not be written down as part of your brainstorming.

Write the topic you chose to brainstorm. Next, list any categories that come to mind. Then list the details under the category to which they belong. If you need more lines than are given, just add them yourself. If you do not have enough details in your brainstorming to fill a category, think of some more now and list them. You don't have to use all of your brainstorming ideas.

Topic _____

Category _____  Category _____  Category _____

_____  _____  _____

_____  _____  _____

_____  _____  _____

_____  _____  _____

# Mapping

The final step of prewriting is developing a map. Mapping is a quick and easy way of putting together similar ideas. That's why it's called a map. The map allows you to see how your ideas are hooked together.

In making a map, you use only key words and phrases, not complete sentences. You start with the *main idea* or topic, placing it in the middle of your paper. *Kinds of Hobbies* on the map below is the topic. To make your topic stand out, you enclose it in some way. Next, lines for the categories are attached to the topic. *Coin Collecting, Model Building*, and *Macrame* are examples on the following map. Finally, the details explaining each category are put on lines that are attached to each category line.

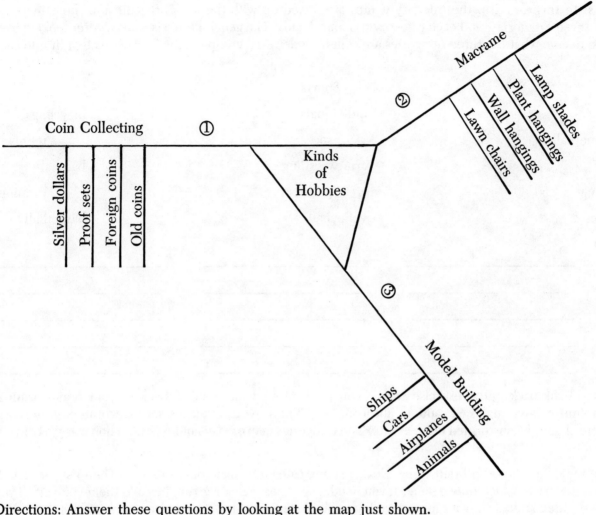

Directions: Answer these questions by looking at the map just shown.

1. What is the topic of the map? _____

2. What are the categories on the map?

_____

_____

_____

3. What are two of the details in category 1?

_____

_____

4. What are two of the details in category 2?

_____

_____

5. What are two of the details in category 3?

_____

_____

Directions: Study this map about a ski trip. Then answer the following questions.

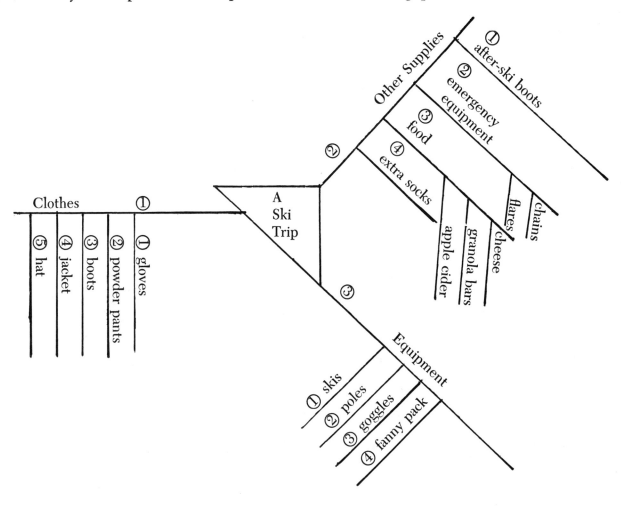

1. What is the topic of this map? _____

2. What are the categories?

3. List some of the details from each category. _____

_____    _____    _____

_____    _____    _____

_____    _____    _____

Directions: Go back to the page where you organized your own brainstorming into categories. Now put the topic, categories, and details for that information on the blank map below. Finally, number the categories and details in an order that makes sense to you.

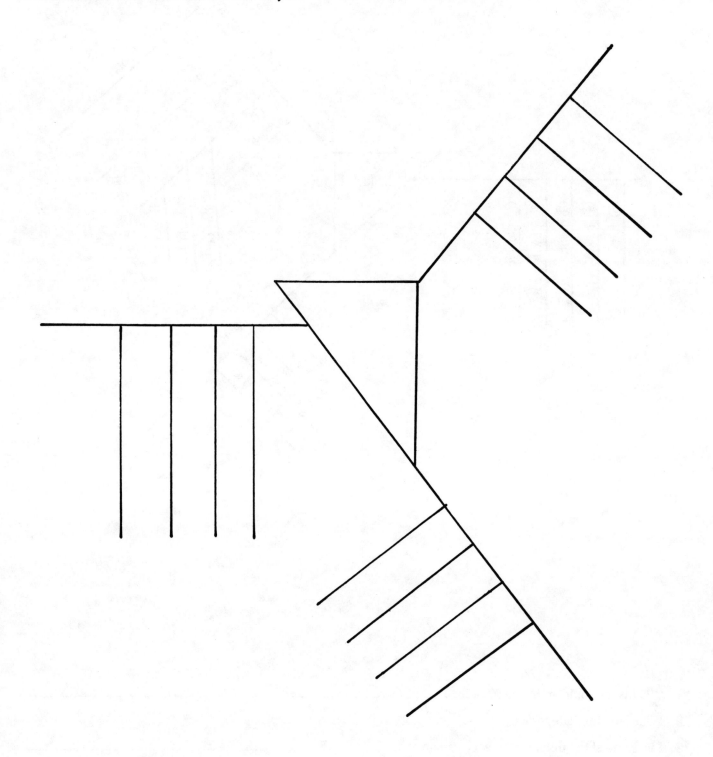

Making a map helps to organize your ideas into paragraphs. Each category and its details represent one paragraph. By numbering the details in the category, you have thought out an order for the ideas within a paragraph.

# The Paragraph

Let's review the definition of a paragraph. A paragraph is a group of sentences about one main idea or topic. Usually, one sentence, called the topic sentence, tells the main idea of the paragraph. All other sentences, in a logical order, explain the topic sentence. A paragraph has three main parts: a topic sentence, supporting or detail sentences, and a concluding sentence.

Directions: Read the following paragraph:

| | |
|---|---|
| Topic sentence | Pizza is my favorite food. First of all, I love mozzarella cheese. I would just as |
| Detail sentences | soon eat mozzarella cheese as go to the new water slide. Also, I love pepperoni. I |
| | like the flavor of pepper and salami. Most of all, I love the thick crust. Of course, |
| | my friends think I'm nuts, but I think that Italian sauce by itself on the crust is |
| Concluding sentence | fantastic. Without pizza, I think I would weigh several pounds lighter. |

This paragraph discusses one main idea: *Pizza is my favorite food.* It contains several supporting or detail sentences. Finally, it ends with a concluding sentence.

Notice the shape of the paragraph. When you begin a paragraph, you signal its beginning to your reader by indenting. Indenting means moving over about one-half inch from the left-hand margin before you write the topic sentence.

Directions: Complete the exercise below by filling in the blanks. This exercise is based on what you have just read about writing.

1. A paragraph is a group of _____ about one _____
   _____ or _____ .

2. Usually, one sentence, called the _____ , tells the _____
   _____ idea.

3. All other sentences _____ the _____
   sentence in a _____ order.

4. A paragraph has _____ main parts:
   a. _____
   b. _____
   c. _____

5. When you begin a paragraph, you _____ its beginning to your reader by
   _____ .

6. Indenting means _____ _____ about
   _____ from the left-hand margin before you write the _____
   _____ _____ .

# The Topic Sentence

The topic sentence has two main functions. The first is to name the paragraph. The second function is to tell the reader what you're going to write about the topic.

Directions: The sentences below are topic sentences. In each sentence, underline the topic. Then circle the key words that tell what the reader is going to be reading about the topic. The first one is done for you.

1. <u>High school</u> students can be divided into three main groups.
2. Summer vacation was a lot of fun.
3. I like rock music for several reasons.
4. Jack's has the best steaks in town.
5. The arcade in the mall is where I go to play my favorite video games.
6. My car and my stereo are my most prized possessions.
7. Although Oregon and California are neighbors, each state has its own characteristics.
8. A pet can help you overcome many problems.
9. Washing my dog is not a pleasant task.
10. Eating candy for lunch can make you excessively active.

Directions: Use the preceding topic sentences. Tell what might be included in the rest of the paragraph. The first two are done for you. Use complete sentences.

1. High school students can be divided into three main groups.

   The rest of the paragraph will explain the three main groups into which high school students are divided.

2. Summer vacation was a lot of fun.

   The rest of the paragraph will explain what events made summer so much fun.

3. I like rock music for several reasons.

   _____

4. Jack's has the best steaks in town.

   _____

5. The arcade in the mall is where I go to play my favorite video games.

   _____

6. My car and my stereo are my most prized possessions.

   _____

7. Although Oregon and California are neighbors, each state has its own characteristics.

   _____

8. A pet can help you overcome many problems.

   _____

9. Washing my dog is not a pleasant task.

_____

10. Eating candy for lunch can make you excessively active.

_____

Don't confuse topic sentences with titles. Remember, a topic sentence tells what the paragraph is about in a complete sentence. A title is seldom a complete sentence. It is usually a fragment or part of a complete thought.

Examples: 1. Title:          Riding a Motorcycle
             Topic Sentence: Riding a motorcycle is not as easy at it looks.

          2. Title:          Starting a New School
             Topic Sentence: Starting a new school can be a frightening experience.

Did you notice the difference in capitalization in the title and in the topic sentence? Several words of a title are capitalized, but only the first word of the topic sentence is capitalized. Be sure your first sentence is your topic sentence when you're learning about writing. Later on, when you become a writing expert, you can experiment by moving the topic sentence around.

Directions: Read the paragraph below, concentrating on the topic sentence.

    Many students enjoy their year at the school because of the many activities. There are sports such as football, volleyball, basketball, and track for the athletes. Some students participate in cheerleading at these events. For others who are politically oriented, there is the school government. The many fantastic assemblies are a great deal of fun, too. Then, of course, there are the terrific dances.

Write the topic sentence of this paragraph:

_____

Directions: Read the groups of sentences below. Each group has one sentence in it that states the main idea of the whole group. It is the topic sentence. Circle the topic sentence in each group.

1. Secondly, they want affection on their own terms.
   For one thing, they'll chase anything that moves.
   If they don't want to be picked up, you can't get near them.
   Cats are funny animals.
   Finally, they're crazy enough to think that they can grab a hummingbird hovering overhead.

2. The Apostle Islands is a great place for a vacation.
   Camping abounds in the many Forest Service campgrounds.
   There's fishing for a large variety of fish.
   With 365 miles of shoreline, there's plenty of room for water skiing.
   You can rent a houseboat and just relax.

3. Mr. Chang, the teacher, keeps the class fun and exciting.
   Taking pictures around the campus is fun, too.
   I love to take pictures of both students and faculty.
   My photography class is great.
   Developing my own pictures is a skill I've always wanted to learn.

Directions: Pick two topics about which you could write a paragraph. Decide what the main idea of each paragraph would be. Then, write a topic sentence for each paragraph that states the main idea.

1. Main Idea: _____

Topic Sentence:

_____

_____

2. Main Idea: _____

   Topic Sentence: _____

_____

Directions: Supply the detail ideas for the topic idea that has already been supplied.

1. TV programs _____ 2. types of cats _____ 3. coins _____

_____     _____     _____

_____     _____     _____

_____     _____     _____

Directions: Now reverse the process that you began in the last exercise. The details are supplied. You come up with a topic idea.

1. _____
   plot
   setting
   time
   character

2. _____
   apples
   oranges
   pears
   bananas

3. _____
   speaker
   tape player
   volume control
   fast forward

4. _____
   preamble
   amendments
   Bill of Rights
   signatures

5. _____
   no gum chewing
   all homework must be in
   always bring a pen
   don't disturb other students

6. _____
   jackets
   warm fires
   hot chocolate
   lots of blankets

Whatever you say in the topic sentence is what you must discuss in your detail sentences. If you have the topic sentence, "My English class is fun because I love to write," then you must discuss your love of writing. If your topic sentence was, "My English class is fun," then you're free to discuss your writing, your teacher, your classmates, and anything else that makes your English class fun.

There is, as a matter of fact, such a thing as saying too much in a topic sentence. Be very general (not specific) in a topic sentence. Leave yourself room to maneuver. Don't limit yourself. Look at this paragraph:

Dogs are good pets, and they bark a lot. They are very loyal. Also, they're good company when you're lonely. Rarely, will they disobey you purposely. Plus, they're nice to cuddle up to when you're cold.

What was missing in the detail sentences that was mentioned in the topic sentence? Right! *Dogs barking a lot.* That's a detail that was made, mistakenly, a part of the topic.

Directions: Look at the topic sentences that follow. In the blanks after the topic sentence, you write *OK* if you think the topic sentences is general enough and *too much* if you think the topic sentence has revealed too much detail. If you think the topic sentence had too much detail, explain why.

1. My little brother is a pest for several reasons.

   _____

2. My room is usually a mess with clothes on the floor and books and papers strewn everywhere.

   _____

3. My favorite story in *Outlooks* is "By the Waters of Babylon" because of the way it's written and, also, I'm against nuclear war.

   _____

4. I like *The Illustrated Man* for a variety of reasons.

   _____

5. We were involved in a lot of activities last summer, like swimming at the lake for one.

   _____

6. There are four important steps in running a computer and the first one is to know how to use software.

   _____

7. Mr. Braithwaite is a neat teacher for several reasons.

   _____

8. My new stereo has a lot of good features like an automatic pause button.

   _____

9. This has been the hottest summer on record.

   _____

10. Some days I feel like doing absolutely nothing.

    _____

11. My dad has got to be the world's greatest storyteller, and he also works for IBM.

    _____

Let's take a look at detail sentences. Those are the sentences that support the topic sentence. They explain it. They detail what you've generalized about in the topic sentence. Suppose you said, "I really thrive on watching cartoons on Saturday morning." There's your topic sentence. A friend might say, "Why?" Now, you must detail why you like cartoons. So, you use detail sentences to explain. In conversation, you'll probably start out with, "Well," and that's okay in speaking. Eliminate it in writing. Here's what you might write:

> I'm captivated by the seemingly unending schemes of Wily Coyote in his pursuit of the Roadrunner. Also, Bugs Bunny has got to be one of the most clever escape artists I've ever seen. He always seems to have a way to elude the stewing pot of Elmer Fudd. Then, there's the famous Tweety Bird and his world renowned "I tot I saw a putty cat." I could watch Saturday morning cartoons all day.

These are all details that support the topic sentence. They explain why. Now, your friend may come back with a topic sentence such as, "I think cartoons are immature." Then, your friend will detail to you why. That's what paragraphs are all about — making a statement and supporting it.

Topic sentences make a general statement without really explaining or saying why. Detail sentences tell why; they explain the topic sentence.

Just as you don't want to say too much in the topic sentence, you don't want to be excessive in your detail sentences and say things that were not introduced in the topic sentence. Look at the following paragraph.

> When I went to the supermarket the other day, I thought that I would die of embarrassment. First of all, when I left the house, I didn't notice the big tear in the rear of my jeans. When I walked into the market, there was Harvey Hiplinger boxing groceries, and anyone knows he's just about the most beautiful human being ever to walk the face of the earth. Next, when I was ready to check out, I picked up the bag and it ripped, dumping groceries all over the floor right in front of Harvey. I could have just died. Incidentally, peaches are on sale this week. Anyway, I gathered up my stuff and got out of there fast.

Which sentence doesn't belong? "Incidentally, peaches are on sale this week." Does that have anything to do with thinking "I would die of embarrassment"? Of course not! So, it shouldn't be included in the details. Remember, what you say in the topic sentence must be what you discuss in the detail sentences.

Directions: In the paragraphs below, there are detail sentences that don't belong. Write them on the spaces provided.

Taking a ride in a hot air balloon is my biggest fantasy. I think I'd enjoy hovering above the city, looking down on the sights below. The noiseless motion of the craft would send shivers of delight through my entire body, just thinking about defying gravity in such simple fashion. Newton discovered gravity, and humans have been trying to overcome it ever since. Also, the fresh, cool air at a higher altitude would be exhilarating.

_____

_____

California has more variety in its landscape than any other state in the nation. If you want the ocean, there's a thousand miles of shoreline. Mountains stretch from one end of the state to the other. There are high deserts and low deserts. Wildlife abounds in all of these places. Big cities like Los Angeles and San Francisco contrast with smaller towns like Peanut and Rough and Ready. Farms dot the landscape of the central valley, while cattle ranches flourish in the north. California is truly a state with many different faces.

_____

_____

There are four steps to remember while driving at night. First of all, drive more slowly. Your braking distance increases because your vision decreases for two reasons: the darkness and the speed. Slow down at night. Secondly, do not stare into the lights of an oncoming car. Keep your eyes focused to the right on the edge of your lane. Bright lights can momentarily blind you even after the oncoming car has passed. Next, watch your gauges. They're the only signs other than smell that will tell you of engine problems. There are some gauges that will give you RPM and others for miles per gallon. Finally, don't overheat the compartment of your car. This is a good way to make yourself drowsy, which is something you want to avoid more than anything else. Keep a window cracked for fresh air to help keep you awake.

_____

_____

There is a standard form for the paragraph. Here is an example:

---

**Paragraph Form**

---

     Paragraph form is simple. First, write your complete heading. Next, center your title on the top line and

---

skip one line. Indent your first line of writing. Each new sentence should begin where the last sentence ends,

---

and you should leave a right-hand margin. In this class, it is required that you skip lines. Finally check for

---

capitals, end marks, and at least five complete sentences.

---

# Rough Draft

     Never plan for the first copy of your paragraph to be your final copy. You almost always need to revise, add to, and correct your work. In your first copy you need to be concerned with getting your ideas down on paper. Don't worry about being totally organized. Don't worry about making everything perfect just yet. Just write.

Directions: Follow the steps to write a rough draft.

**Step 1:** To begin writing your rough draft, look at your preprinting map. Decide the category about which you're most interested in writing. You already have numbered your details, but look at that order again. Does it still make sense to you? You will be writing your detail sentences in the order in which you have numbered them. Make a change now, if you wish.

Now look at the topic in the middle of your map. Write the topic here: _____.

Next, look at the category you've chosen to write about. Write the category name here: _____

_____. The words you've put on these two blanks are the topic and key words, and these

ideas should all be included in your topic sentence.

**Step 2:** Write two topic sentences that fit your topic and category. Remember, the topic sentence states the main idea of your paragraph. It tells your reader what you're going to write about but doesn't give specific details.

1. _____

   _____

2. _____

   _____

**Step 3:** Begin the rough draft of your paragraph by indenting and writing the topic sentence you've chosen to use. Continue using paragraph form. Do not indent again; begin each new sentence where the one before it ends. Go back to the proper paragraph form.

**Step 4:** Look at your map. Find the detail you've marked as number 1. This idea should now be explained in a detail sentence or two. Be sure it makes sense with your topic sentence.

**Step 5:** Next, write a detail sentence or two explaining each of the details that you marked as numbers 2, 3, and 4.

**Step 6:** Finally, you should write a concluding sentence. A concluding sentence puts the finishing touch on your paragraph. It can either restate the main idea in your topic sentence using different wording, or it can make a final comment about what you have said in your paragraph. You should make your concluding sentence interesting.

**Step 7:** At this point, you should put your rough draft away for one whole day. By doing this, you will more easily catch some of your own errors before it is rewritten and edited by other students.

# Postwriting
# Revision: Rewriting and Editing

Congratulations! You've just written the first draft of your paragraph. This rough draft lets you see your paragraph in complete sentences and paragraph form for the first time. However, you are not yet finished. Remember, this first draft of your paragraph is rough (partially done and incomplete). The third and one of the most important stages of writing — revising — is still ahead.

Revising is more than just correcting spelling and punctuation errors. It is looking at your paper again, deciding what is and isn't good about it, and making as many changes as are needed so that your paragraph is the best it can be. Good writers don't mind revising, because they want their words to communicate exactly what they want to say.

Just as authors revise (rewrite and edit) their work before sending it to a publisher, you as a student writer need to revise your work before handing it in for grading. Good writing always includes rewriting, no matter how good your map is, no matter how long you've already spent writing, no matter how smart you are, and no matter how neat your rough draft is. One draft isn't enough.

# Editing

Editing, cleaning up and correcting a piece of writing, is a skill that has to be learned. A good editor becomes good by practicing and by wanting to do a good job.

By doing the exercises that follow, you will have a chance to improve your editing expertise before you actually work on another student's papers. The exercises will help you to be aware of the types of errors you should be looking for in your own paper and in those of others. You'll be doing exercises in capitalization, sentence fragments, spelling, and punctuation. So, review your skills in these areas.

# Editing: Capitalization

Directions: A coded message is hidden in the paragraph below. Correct the capitalization in the typed paragraph, circling the capital letters. If you capitalized correctly, the circled letters will form the coded message.

perry intune asked his father, "can you give me $300?"

ken intune, perry's dad, replied, "until your chores are done, we won't discuss money, perry. friday is your allowance day, i think, anyway. Three hundred dollars! very funny!"

eagerly, perry pursued, "I want to go to bend, oregon, and then into nevada, utah, and south dakota with my archaeology class."

"perry," his dad replied, "that's fine, but you must earn that kind of money. times are changing. seems like when I was a kid, we had to earn the money for that sort of thing. Besides, if you want to study something old, talk to me."

Secret message: _ _ _ _ _ _ _ _ _ _ _ _ _ _ _ _ _ _ _ _ _ _ _ _ _ _ _ —.

# Editing: Sentence Fragments

Directions: The paragraph below contains sentence fragments. Rewrite the paragraph, changing the fragments to complete sentences. Draw a line under the topic sentence. Indent your paragraph.

Downhill skiing. This can be a great sport. And a wonderful way to get some valuable exercise. One of the best benefits of this sport is being in the high altitude fresh air. Which does wonders for clearing out your stuffed sinuses and lungs. Also, the views are fantastic. With the beautiful white snow on the ground and the gorgeous evergreen trees cast against the blue of the seemingly endless sky. It seems as though you become so hypnotized by the super scenery. That you don't even notice your muscles being challenged as you work your way down the slope. It's a good tired feeling though. Because you know you've been exercising and stretching your muscles all day long. By the end of the day. You know that you've received the benefits of exercise in an atmosphere that has also been very relaxing.

_____

_____

_____

_____

_____

# Editing: Spelling

Directions: Correct the spelling errors in the paragraph below. There are twenty-four errors.

Country liveing offers a teenager alot of diffrent activities. Riding bicks on durt trails is probly one of the most popular sports in the area. Boating on a lake is fun, to. With it's many miles of shoreline, their's room to swim, fish, water ski, etc. Becuse of the heat in the summer, just lieing out in the sun is a vary common recreation. Its alright not to get a tan just as long as you soke up the sunshine. Too other grate activities in are super area our horseback rideing and tenis. They're is a variety of things to due in the country.

_____

_____

_____

_____

_____

# Editing: Punctuation

Directions: In the paragraph below, there are errors in commas, periods, and quotation marks. Rewrite the paragraph, correcting the punctuation errors. Here are the number of errors you should find: commas — fourteen, periods — five and quotation marks — two.

If you want to have an educational afternoon visit the Shasta Historical Society museum in Redding California. In it you'll find many items of interest One of the most unique is a letter written by Major Pierson B Reading He wrote it to his daughter in the late 1800's. He tells her Please be careful in your travels to Weaverville California as I hear tell of many marauders in that area." He goes on to say, "It would be advisable to carry a weapon Another article of interest especially to the girls is an old-fashioned curling iron. This was heated for several minutes atop a wood-burning stove. For more information on the museum write to Richard Eaton president Shasta Historical Society General Delivery Redding California 96001

_____

_____

_____

_____

_____

# Peer Editing

Peer editing is having your fellow students read your paper and help you improve it. It can be very hard for you to catch your own errors, either because you don't know it's an error at all, or because when you read your paper, you read it the way you meant it instead of seeing the mistake. Having others check your paper for you is a very important step in turning out the best possible paper you can.

As you practice editing other students' papers, always remember that your aim is to help as much as possible. Any comments or corrections you make should be thoughtful and clear. Take time to read and think about the paper carefully. If you're not sure about something the writer says or of something that might or might not need revision, ask the person who wrote the paper or ask the teacher. Don't be afraid to make suggestions and to ask questions. Make a special point to say something good about each paper.

When you have your paper edited by other students, be sure you understand what they have said about and done with your paper. Remember, you don't have to take anyone's suggestions — but, if a true error is pointed out, be sure that you correct it.

When you edit someone else's paper, you should use a different color ink, or if he or she wrote in ink, you can use pencil. This way your corrections stand out.

After having your paper edited, you need to go over it carefully. Make any needed corrections, ask those who edited your paper about any suggestions or corrections that you don't understand, and then hand your paragraph in for teacher correction. At this point, your paper only needs to be recopied if it is quite messy and difficult to read.

After your teacher checks your paper, you may need to recopy it. However, you don't have to recopy if you can correct your errors neatly. Don't be afraid to make changes with a pen if you notice mistakes. As long as the corrections are neatly made, your teacher probably won't consider it messy. Just remember, your corrected, final copy should be well packaged — clean, neat, legible ink copy that is easy to read. Proofread your paper one last time before handing it in for your final grade.